INTERSECTIONS

NICKI SALCEDO

Intersections
By Nicki Salcedo
Dan Whisenhunt, Editor
Dena Mellick, Associate Editor
Copyright © 2015 by Nicki Salcedo

Some names and identifying details have been changed to protect the privacy of individuals.

The pieces in this collection were originally published on the websites Decaturish.com, It's Only a Novel, and Petit Fours and Hot Tamales.

Cover art licensed through canstockphoto.com, copyright © Lirch

Cover design: Shane Milburn

Tags 1. American wit and humor 2. Southern 3. Essays 4. Motherhood 5. Life lessons

ISBN: 0996541802
ISBN-13: 978-0-9965418-0-0

DEDICATION

To SRS, EJS, NAS, IES

The world is kind. The world is good. Sometimes you have to look for the good. Sometimes the good will find you. All my love.

CONTENTS

CONTENTS (CONTINUED)

FOREWORD

By Dan Whisenhunt

I first heard about Nicki Salcedo when I read about her in the news.

My day-job is editing and publishing Decaturish.com. My real job is trying to find time to write and run a business. One day, one of our talented contributors – Mr. Ralph Ellis – pitched a story to me about a Decatur woman who had published her first novel, titled *All Beautiful Things*.

Ellis wrote that for Nicki, "Taking care of four kids, ages 3-10, and holding down a job as an account executive makes it a challenge to find writing time."

"Now a lot of it happens on the weekend," Nicki told Ellis. "I write at soccer games, while my kids are at piano lessons, while I wait in the doctor's office."

Finding time in the margins to write is something I know a little bit about.

A coincidence brought Nicki into my world. We were both celebrating our graduation from the Decatur 101 Class, a Public Relations seminar masquerading as civic education. We were sharing a drink at the bar in Eddie's Attic. We got free coupons for completing the course. After it dawned on me that she was the subject of Ralph's article and it dawned on her that I published Decaturish, we hit it off.

I found Nicki to be down to earth and naturally funny. We both realized we had a mutual admiration and respect for columnist Lewis Grizzard.

How we got on the topic of a regular column I couldn't quite tell you. It wasn't a hard sell. I know we hammered out the details of it over coffee a few days later and soon "Intersections" became a weekly feature.

Some of my readers, particularly the male ones, tell me they don't "get" Nicki's columns. They come to

Decaturish looking for news, and Nicki's columns are not about the news. They are her feelings, observations and ideas about her personal experiences.

My usual response to her critics is, "She's not writing for you. She's writing for people who don't normally read the news." Whether you "get" Nicki or not, the numbers don't lie. Her columns are widely-read and shared often. She's gained a devoted following, including people who might not otherwise read Decaturish. Nicki broadens our reach and provides a voice that's truly unique.

Her columns are also a pleasure to edit. Nicki's one of the few writers who can complete my sentences. I can give her vague advice like, "You need to tighten up the writing a bit" and she knows exactly what I'm talking about. Some writers don't give you much to work with. Nicki's problem is the opposite. She gives you an abundance. As an old theater director of mine once put it, it's easier to push someone back down a well than to pull them out of it. My job with her columns is to take something that's already pretty good and make it awesome. Editing it is something I look forward to every week. I'm like a fan with VIP access.

I guess it doesn't hurt that we also share a mutual interest in *Star Trek* and *Star Wars*, but it probably wouldn't matter if we didn't. A good writer commands respect, even you don't identify with them completely.

I've got mad respect for Nicki Salcedo. Her writing engages the senses and her voice is genuine. Her writing is deeply personal, warm and giving. She leaves nothing on the table. Her words are weighted with wisdom. Her column never leaves me feeling empty.

Like Nicki, this compilation of her work has a lot to offer. If it were a video game, I'd say it has a lot of replay value.

Keep this book close by for those moments when you need a smile or a little inspiration. Sometimes you can find it in the most unlikely places, like in the voice of a

Southern woman born in Jamaica who has a fondness for Lewis Grizzard.

Whether you "get" Nicki or not, you've got to admit that there's no one quite like her.

- Dano

INTERSECTIONS

I'm not a storyteller. I don't tell stories. Stories tell me. I've been told I'm not Southern, because I'm not Southern by birth or ancestry. But I want to be. I've lived here, some easy striking distance from Atlanta most of my life. There were those San Francisco years. I admit it. I left and brought my heart back with me. I came back for the trees and the grass and the stories.

Now I'm home-ish. My husband, that heart from California, accepts my pronunciation of Ponce de Leon with some skepticism. I think my way is right for Georgia. I accept the fact that when I say "Ponce" I am wrong. And right. His way for the person. My way for the street. My life is full of intersections. These intersections are stories, so I must be just a little bit Southern. This is how I know.

I walk slowly. I hug the magnolia tree in front of the Decatur Library. I like football and baseball. I can hear the difference between a foul ball and a homerun. I like to walk in the cemetery, not for history, but the unexpected sound of laughter and the menace of geese. I like romance and time travel. I don't want to belong to any one thing. Even this town. My entire life is an intersection.

I pause too long at the place where two roads meet. Any direction could be the right choice. Sometimes I don't choose. I merely stand in place and wonder which way to go. My kids don't stand still. There are four of them. Outnumbered does not accurately describe what happens to us against them. They are all smiles, but he and I have the last laugh.

I hear stories everywhere. I've struggled with tragedy. Fire and loss and cancer. I cried for people I knew and others I didn't. I looked for happiness in the world, and when I couldn't find it I made my own.

I see stories everywhere. In the post office, the woman behind the counter spoke to a customer with infinite patience. All the other customers were agitated, but the old lady took her time buying stamps. The employee smiled at her. Why should that kindness surprise me? I'm sure there is a story there. I'm sure there is a reason, a story, for why I was surprised.

A woman hurried down the street, Ponce de Leon Avenue, and into the yoga studio. The rush to meditate is not unusual. I first noticed her blue yoga mat. It was weathered and faded. She hurried with her blue mat, but wore red stiletto heels. I'm sure there was a story there. What I love best about the South is the constant intersection of things that seemingly don't match.

Stories find us even when we aren't looking or listening or waiting at intersections. I've been told I'm not Southern, but I am just a little bit. I like pollen better than snow. I tell stories and stories tell me. Here, we are past the Ides of April, and it is very cold. Spring and winter are married for the day. My car is frozen and covered in pollen. These things don't match, but I like them.

If you see me around town looking lost, don't worry. I'm wondering about things that don't go together. West and South. Snow and pollen. Stilettoes and yoga mats. I'm that not-quite-Southern girl at the intersection. If I wait long enough, the stories will tell me which way to go.

SOME DANCE TO REMEMBER

When we buried my father-in-law I didn't cry. He died too young, too suddenly, and his passing elicited too many feelings. None of the emotions were subtle like sadness. I was angry at him for leaving my kids without their grandpa. They loved him. Because they loved him, and he left them, I was angry. I couldn't cry. I believed for a moment if I was angry enough we could get him back.

When we landed in San Francisco that week, the first song we heard was "Hotel California" by the Eagles. It brought a smile to my face on a day when I didn't think I could smile.

"On a dark desert highway, cool wind in my hair..."

I can't say that I'm a fan of the Eagles. But I know a few of their songs. I'm the wrong generation and wrong demographic, but one particular lyric stood out as we drove on the dark deserted highway between Gilroy and Salinas.

"Some dance to remember. Some dance to forget."

It struck me that was the reason I enjoy reading and writing so much. The answer was in the Eagles. Some write to remember. Some write to forget.

I write to remember. Writing is a recollection of things that startle your senses. You might remember that air in California is different, but you will write about the scent of eucalyptus interrupted with the stench of skunk. Or that the

3

sand-peppered wind is as chilling as the frigid waves. You write because you can't find anyone who makes tortillas the way your grandmother used to make and you want to remember. You write because touching your husband's hand on a cold winter's morning is not the same as touching his father's lifeless hand, but the similarity is painfully present. Some write to forget.

Sometimes I write to forget. I read to disappear. I hope to lessen the pain. Writing takes me back to places that are lost by time or distance.

"We haven't had that spirit here since nineteen sixty-nine."

Whenever I meet people, I tell them they should write. I always have a spare book in my house or my bag that I can share with a friend or a stranger.

I write with hope. I hope the air smells like lovely eucalyptus or wintry pine. I hope my husband will always remember the taste of his grandmother's homemade tortillas. I hope to remember the grudging look of approval my father-in-law gave me when he first met me, and I spent three days making tamales with my mother-in-law. I hope to always remember that. Some dance to forget. Some dance to remember.

TOP DOWN

Spring worries me, because it leads to more illness than cold weather. I have stock in allergy medicine. Pollen covers everything. I only have one friend who drives a convertible in Atlanta. We have plenty of sunshine, but we aren't a city of convertible cars. Not like L.A. Not much pollen there. Less rain. Our cars in Georgia have proper roofs and rightly so. What would my mother say if she saw me with my top down? She raised me better than that. At most, we are sunroof people, no matter the season.

I opened my sunroof the other day. That square foot of sunshine and air looked like a video screen. I'm either all inside (work) or all outside (soccer mom), but hardly ever both at the same time. When I opened the sunroof, a green inch worm tried to climb in. I shut the roof before it could parachute down. Now, I am not a convertible person or a sunroof person. The outside—moss and pollen and caterpillars—needs to stay out.

Maybe I should feel ashamed of hiding in my mini-van kingdom. If it's not covered in pollen, the dirt and dust keeps us coated all year. I can't figure out when to wash it. All washing does is bring forth rain and snow and pollen. The inside is no better. My kids have found ways to terrorize me even when they aren't in the car.

A single soccer ball rolls around in the back seat. A half-full jug of water swishes around in the trunk. It unnerves me as I drive, but when I get home I immediately forget about it. It's been back there for a month.

When I put the windows down, the wind picks up loose bits of paper in the car. Empty granola bar wrappers and last week's homework rise off the floor. Pieces of our life dance in the rearview window. This happens all the time. Windows down and suddenly everything is weightless. Empty chip bags, piano music, and unfinished artwork stay afloat in the wind like I've reversed gravity. Thanks, kids. They know I like *Star Trek*. Might as well turn my mini-van into the Enterprise.

I boldly go to work and school and soccer. I scatter squirrels and errant birds and new life forms and civilizations. Pollen blows against my windshield. I use the wipers to clear my view, but it looks like I'm whirling through space.

Last year, my convertible friend took me on a drive and for a moment it was California dreaming on Atlanta's I-285. I'm sure she is sad for my mini-van life. I hadn't felt the wind in my face since . . . ever. We were all sunshine and air and smiles. No caterpillars tried to hitch a ride.

Her kids are grown and gone, but mine are still being carried in my kangaroo pouch, the mini-van. It does not have much sunshine or wind, but it has sounds and magic and free rides for inch worms, as long as the inch worms stay outside.

THE SCENT OF PENCILS AND PINE

There are mornings when I wake up next to a man I do
not recognize. On my finger, I see his ring, plain white gold
that is slightly dented instead of inscribed. This band is the
only indication that I am his and he is mine.

I close my eyes and inhale. Then my eyes open slowly, and
I realize that I do know him. I know his scent.

He sleeps the way men do, deeply generating heat that has
a gravitational pull. He is in another world. I sleep like a cat,
with one eye open. If he ever thought to wake and gaze at
me, I would know instantly. But he sleeps soundly, journeys
to distant dimensions, and I can watch him at my leisure
before he wakes.

I close my eyes again and inhale. When I was young and
foolish I told him that he smelled like sand and tasted like the
ocean. How else do you compliment a boy from California?
Things like the ocean and eucalyptus were foreign to me then.
I grew up with Georgia. My oceans were forests—deep, lush,
and green even in the cold of winter. Even now, I'm so
familiar with the scent of pine I don't notice it.

When I first met him it was like seeing the ocean. He was
both wild and calming. When he first met me he said I
smelled like freshly-sharpened pencils. I didn't know then
what he meant, but I do now. He knows me not because I

smell like pencils, but because I smell like pine.

I don't compliment him on his scent anymore. We are not in that kind of love anymore, but I still think he is delicious. He smells better than peach cobbler or pot roast, but I don't tell him. These are not things he should know.

Each morning he enfolds me in his arms. We have to be brief in our touches. Each moment is a precursor to the cat purring and staring at us upside-down, or a child crying and wanting to join our snuggles.

All day we are absent from each other. How many things come between us? The distance, welcome or dreaded, is unavoidable. The world is filled with scents I dislike. Exhaust, tar, burnt popcorn. Sometimes I smell good things. Paper warm from the printer or the last fresh scent flowers give before the bouquet dies.

At the end of the day, we are reunited. I find my offspring – the other halves of him – and they are syrupy with their stickiness and unnatural heat. When he arrives there is an unexplainable buzz of erratic running and then we fall into hugs. We are a family of wild cubs. What else should we do other than sniff each other and laugh?

He leaves us to make dinner, and he roasts green chilies on a cast iron pan. The fire is hot. We feel it from across the kitchen. He pulls back the transparent pepper skin to create food the way he learned from his female ancestors. His mother three times zones away would be proud. Because his grandmother is no longer alive, she can be nearer. Her ghostly hands, wrinkled though softened with lard and masa, guide him. The way he touches food is hypnotic. It reminds me of how he touches me.

The chilies under his care are not diminished. Their aroma lingers. It reminds us that it came from the earth.

We don't wash dishes. We don't have time. We'd rather spend our time sitting next to the tub getting splashed or turning our noses into necks. But the truth of the world is never this ideal. Nothing is perfection.

His feet stink. His big toe has a monster nail that scratches me in the night. He snores and sleeps with his mouth open. I dodge his wayward elbows. I am not perfect either. Sometimes I make mean faces, and I want to be alone. Sometimes I am too tired to bathe. Sometimes I want to smell like the real me. The me of pine and pencils.

His scent varies. Today it is foreign, and I don't recognize him. Diaper ointment. Laundry detergent. He will do blasphemous things like use soap and add deodorant and cologne. He will put on suits and ties and discard his holey shorts and flip flops. Gone will be the stranger and my clean, well-dressed husband will arrive. He carries a briefcase, but he still listens to his music too loud.

When I am unsure of who he is or who I am, I let him embrace me. I smell him. His sweat is sweet. When he laughs I laugh with him. I inhale and he inhales back. He can tell when I am wanting, when I am pregnant, when I am sad. I can tell him from any other creature. Sometimes he purrs. Sometimes he too cries out for my attention. Deep in the pine forest where we live, I know him. His scent still reminds me of sand. He still tastes like the ocean.

A LETTER TO MY CHILDREN

I I don't trust memoir. It always rings false. The idea that my life might hold someone's interest is unlikely, but there might be snippets, short eras that can entrance like fiction. Ironically, I always wished my mother had chronicled her life. I always thought my father's mother might have been healed by telling her secrets. Or his. Those before me were not raised to glorify their tragedies or jinx their hopes and dreams. If their curse was to be silenced, then our curse is to expose too much. My words, pictures, moving images will also be lost, but not for lack of being told. My stories will be lost because they are being told in a forest dense and electronic. A silence made of white noise.

I am writing to you, my children, so you can know a little about me.

Where I'm From.

I was born on an island called Jamaica. For the first two years of my life, I…I don't know what. I don't remember. If this were memoir, I would say something about the scent of hibiscus or the quiet heat of the night and the opposing coolness rising from the tiled floor. I would tell you that when I heard a helicopter or airplane, I would run to my Vava, my grandfather, and it was the only time I would let him hold me. But those are not my memories. Those memories belong to someone else.

What I knew of Jamaica I learned in America. Jamaica was food. Jamaica was accents my friends could detect, but I could not. To my friends, my parents' voices were spicy, rapid, and strange. To me, my parents sounded like air. If their voices had a flavor it would have been water.

If Jamaicans were in the news or in sports, my family paid attention. We were proud of gold medals. We noted news stories of Jamaicans rising to positions of prominence in America and in the world. Even a singsong commercial from the tourism board would cause my family to pause. We would watch an idealized version of a land that was no longer ours.

I often wondered why my parents left an island where they had a nice house in the hills overlooking the capital city. They were not wealthy, but they were comfortable. I wondered what I would have been like if I sounded like my parents. If I could remember. If I had grown up on that island. Why they left is not my story to tell, but I know that they left with a sense that by leaving they could give their children, my sisters and I, different and possibly better opportunities.

As a young child in America, I had many friends who were born in places like Korea, Columbia, and India. We all felt the same. Wholly American and yet different enough to not quite belong. I have recognized my own limbo and yearning to belong in the words of authors like Maxine Hong Kingston and Sandra Cisneros. It did not matter to me if they were Jamaican, just that we, inwardly, were the same.

Who I am.

Americans are dreamers. It is for this reason that I write my letter to you today. Dreaming is who we are, but I was never one of those girls who dreamed of being married or imagined having babies. When I was growing up, I did all of my dreaming for fictional characters. Characters I read in books, and eventually characters I created.

I love happily ever after. I love romance. I love that dreaming is ingrained into the culture of this country. For me dreaming is imagining new stories.

But now I have to dream a little dream for you.

I dream that you will understand that you are not the center of the universe, but on a small blue planet in the corner and the rest are burning bright red to white-hot. I dream that you will one day be able to take care of yourself, your family, and your world. I dream that you won't look to anyone else to take care of you. As your mother, that is my job. If I have done it well, no one else need take care of you save your father. His wisdom is different, maybe even greater, but he leaves the writing to me.

This is what you need to know about me. I believe that laughter and desolation are roommates. I smile at strangers. I get mad at those I love best. I am wrong sometimes. I still don't think of myself as a mother. I like laughing. I accept anger. I like being around people who are different from me. I like science fiction and the Bible. I like football and poetry.

I have fallen in love and gotten married. I have had the happiest of days. I've given birth and miscarried. I have had the most desolate of days curled up in bed, the room pungent with the smell of blood and also the sweet scent of amniotic fluid. I'll never be done. I'm learning every day like you are learning.

Are the things I'm telling you really me? I don't know. I worry that you may never really know me because I will filter all that I am into fiction. I write because it makes me happy. Even when I write about sad things it improves my spirit. Ask me. Talk to me. I will try to tell what you want to know when you need to know it.

My wish for you?

I wish my grandmother could have told me her story. My flippant American girl ways irritated her. When I asked her about her life, she would cry. I don't know my grandmother's story, but I imagine she was filled with shame for events seventy years forgotten, but not forgotten by her.

I still want my mother to write me a letter. I want to hear her happy stories and stories about her dreams, even if they were deferred.

I wish you many things: struggle and heartache and happiness. They are unavoidable.

I would tell you that I love you, but you know this. I wash behind your ears. I clip your toenails. I wish I cleaned better or cooked better, but I don't. I only know how to share books with you. Sometimes we look at a bunny looking at the moon and back, and you get the idea. There is no end to this, and that is something to rejoice in. Your stories and mine together make a new story. And so it will be with your children.

I am so thankful that my parents took a risk and changed their world for me. Enjoy what has been given to you. Every day the world will change for you if you give back a little more than you have received.

DON'T READ THE COMMENTS

I'm sure your mother told you it's impolite to talk about politics, religion, and sex. She was right in a way. If you talk about it, you have to endure the comments.

I don't ever talk politics. I trust no one. I vote. I don't complain. I don't even like talking politics with those who agree with my politics (more *Star Trek*, more romance novels, more fresh air).

I have a surprising number of friends who are my political opposite. I think I need to wear more shirts that say "Anarchy" or "Make Love Not War." The truth is I like to surround myself with lots of different types of people and in my life sometimes different means opposite. Sports fans get together for the love of the sport even if they are cheering on different teams. We should take that spirit into politics. I wish more people talked about politics. We should be like sports fans.

It's not the debate that worries me. It's the lack of respect. We need the ability to understand one view and at the same time try to understand the counterpoint. I love *Star Trek*, but then right away the *Star Wars* people assume I'm against them. I'm not. I'm Pro-Wookie.

When it comes to my faith, I tend to be quiet like I am with my politics. I have a friend who spent every week of a year visiting different places of worship whether or not the place of worship reflected her religious tradition. She wasn't afraid that experiencing another religion would draw her away from her current beliefs. For me learning about other religions reinforces my beliefs. I can learn something from everyone. I have respect for another person's spiritual practice or lack of. My friends who choose to be free of a faith tradition don't lack compassion. I learn from them, but I disagree when they say religions are screwed up. Religions are fine. People screw up religion. Humans are great at taking great ideas and turning them into sausage. The bad kind of sausage.

Religion is about closing your eyes and knowing the world is still there, flawed and perfect. Religion is the best of a mystery, fantasy, and spy novel wrapped into one and turned into a self-help book. If you don't have a religion, you should try one. If you don't need one, don't bash them.

Politics and religion are communal and worthy of discussion, but sex is not communal (Please don't give me examples to the contrary. I know about them.). Sex is private, and there are the reasons we don't talk about sex. Let's talk about it.

But, wait. Your mother was right: Do not talk about sex. It's like the first and second rules of *Fight Club*. My doctor keeps explaining this "theory" about where babies come from. I'm pretty sure my doctor is wrong. I don't want to talk or hear about sex.

At its best, it is a mutual pleasure, a comedy, or a thanksgiving. At its worst, sex can be angry, hurtful, an act of dominance or desperation, a plea, or a false sense of connection. We don't talk about sex because the word is loaded with too many conflicting connotations.

But then again, maybe we should talk about sex. When I look at magazine articles describing 25 ways to do it, they don't tell you that:

1. Sex is how you make babies (if you believe that).
2. There are really only four ways to do it and the rest

are just flourishes.

3.   What you are really looking for is not better sex, but better love.

How to make love? You don't want advice from me. I'll tell you to sleep in separate twin beds like Lucy and Desi did. They were still able to make a baby! Sex is one hour a day, and love is 23 hours of the day. You need the recipe for Love? I made this for a friend just before she got married, but you can make it any time you need love. Sometimes it comes in handy to have a recipe when you've forgotten how to do it.

Recipe for Love

Please do not make Love in the bedroom. You should only make Love in the kitchen as with all other recipes.

Ingredients:
1 Quick kiss goodbye in the morning
1 "Have a good day, [insert term of endearment]"
1-2 Conversations, emails, messages that end with "I love you" during the day
1 "I'm happy to see you" at the end of the day
1 "Tell me about your day"
1 Playful touch during dinner that has nothing to do with sex
1 X-rated kiss before bed that has everything to do with sex (even if you are too tired or have too much work to do to even think about having sex)

Directions:
To make Love add more of each ingredient as needed. Learn to appreciate the sunshine and rain. Laugh at yourselves. Try to make Love as often as possible. No need to cool. Love should be (and is often best when) served hot! Make Love every day. Yield two servings.

Sex, politics, and religion are some of my favorite things to talk about. We are nicer in person. More cordial. I might read up on these topics, but I never read the comments. Just because we can say something doesn't mean we should.

NATIVITY

When I found out I was pregnant with my fourth child the message did not come from an angel, but a little plastic pregnancy test. Actually, three pregnancy tests because I couldn't believe I was pregnant again. My three older children were finally at an almost manageable stage when I found out we would have one more.

I am not ashamed to tell you I cried when I found I was going to have another baby. I had recently started a new job. I was working on my third novel and revising another. I had laundry to do. I had dishes to wash. I was scared. I was afraid that I couldn't be a good mother to a fourth child. Reason told me that I could not handle anymore disorder. What would happen to that fourth little baby in all our chaos? I kept thinking, "I can't do this. I can't. I can't manage as it is. How can I manage more?"

On top of that, my doctor considered me "advanced maternal age." That means I'm old, and they wanted to heap worrisome tests on a mother who worried when things were fine. If worry was an Olympic sport, I could gold medal in it. My husband and I agreed to forgo the extra tests. And wait. And while I waited I did what I'd done the three pregnancies before that: I was sick every day. Not morning sick, but morning-afternoon-night sick. Not only first trimester sick, but sick until the day I delivered. And I waited for that day.

Twelve days before Christmas, I gave birth to a baby who came into the world quietly. It snowed all day. I took that as a good omen, but days later I was very sick and back in the hospital. Without my baby. While I knew that I needed to get better, I also knew that I needed to get back to my kids.

On December 23, I told the doctor I was leaving the hospital. I missed my kids. I needed to see them. Even now reflecting on it, my body braces for the pain of their absence. Two days before Christmas, I got to go home.

That night after everyone went to sleep, I sat by the Christmas tree with the baby. I held her to my breast. Instead of feeling close to my baby, I felt close to someone long ago named Mary.

Maybe no one thought it worthwhile to document her worry or fear. It is possible that she was sick during her pregnancy and the trip to Bethlehem exhausting. Maybe the manger was the last straw for her. Maybe she was filled with doubt and "I can't do this." More likely she was stronger than me, more cheerful and more patient. The moment I looked down at my child, I felt a voice inside of me saying, "I can." I felt a trembling happiness unlike any other I'd felt before. Maybe Mary felt that way.

I thought about my mother holding me as a child. I thought about my mother's mother. I thought of my mother-in-law and my sisters. I thought about how each of us was once someone's miracle. And that miracles are born despite fear and difficulties.

Do you know the circumstances of your birth? Was it lowly and in a manger? Did you have a good mother? Did you struggle? Maybe you are adopted. Maybe you will choose to not have children. Maybe you cannot find meaning in a Nativity story. I hope you do.

The circumstances of your birth and what you will become aren't always related. The road to Bethlehem was difficult, but now, wherever you are, you are a miracle.

Merry Christmas.

THANK YOU, BALTIMORE

I think I'm supposed to have a grudge against Baltimore. But when I arrive, I can't remember if it's because of baseball or football. I don't hold grudges for long.

I'm in the Convention Center. It's the end of the day when your feet hurt, and your suit is too constricting, and you just want to lie down and go to sleep because you're too tired to eat or drink.

That's me.

Today is one of those days.

Somewhere in the masses a baby is crying.

I walk with my friends. I look back and see a woman carrying a child. My friends and I keep walking. Our hotel is about a mile away through the maze of exhibit halls and skywalks.

We walk for five minutes hearing crying. I'm a mother. I don't like the sound. I accept it, but I don't like it. We get to an elevator and the crying in the distance stops. I tell my friends I'm used to the sound of crying. But I'm not.

At the next floor, we continue our walk. We still have another half a mile ahead of us when we run into another friend. We stop and talk for a moment. The elevator opens and the crying starts again.

I see a mom. She is pregnant. She carries a toddler girl on

her hip. The girl is crying. Next to the mother a little boy walks. The mother puts down her large shopping bag and asks the boy to carry it. The bag is very big, and he begins to drag it.

There are approximately 2,000 professional people filing past the pregnant lady with the two children. I tell my friends I'll meet them at the hotel. I go to the boy and pick up the bag. We start walking.

"Thank you," the mother says.

I think she is French, but I'm not sure. Her accent tells me she is not from Baltimore. She is model tall and waif thin, except for that pregnant belly. The girl is still crying against her mother's chest. The mother's face is free of makeup, but she is pretty. I do not look her in her eyes. I feel terribly embarrassed.

I smile at that boy, and he starts talking to me. I'm wearing a neon-pink down coat. It's 30 degrees outside, the end of winter. He has just been to the aquarium. Instead of Dora the Explorer, the boy likes Dora's cousin Diego. The one who rescues animals.

"I like Diego too," I say. He is five years old and pure happiness. If I had not turned back, the boy would have dragged the bag for his mom.

We walk for a long time. Pregnant women carrying toddlers walk very slowly. Little tired boys walk very slowly. Only the boy speaks.

Eventually, we get to their hotel. My hotel is six blocks in the opposite direction. We stand in the lobby waiting for the elevator.

"I have four kids," I say. This is the first time I speak to the mother. "I used to look just like you, pregnant, carrying a kid, and others trailing behind."

Suddenly her eyes fill with tears.

The boy reaches up and absent-mindedly touches his sister's foot. The mother now carries the girl straddled over her pregnant belly. She has wrapped both arms around the girl.

"I think we should have taken a taxi," she says. These are her second words to me. I remember seeing the aquarium all the way across the harbor. My feet hurt for them. I felt like crying too. My own eyes fill with tears.

"How old are your kids?" she asks quietly. Through her tears she smiles.

"Eight, seven, five, and two. People think I'm lucky when I travel. That I get to sleep alone in a hotel room. But I miss my kids. I'd rather have my kids with me and crying than be away from them. And we have a rule in my house. Crying is okay."

She nods. She is crying, but her expression is still smiling. Why isn't it okay for us to cry? The adults?

We reach their floor. The 14th. There is no 13th floor.

"We also have a lot of fun," I say. This is true. In our house, we both cry and laugh.

We reach the hotel room. I put down the bag at the door and walk away. I don't wait for her to find her key. The boy continues to talk to his mother, his sister, the air. I never ask him his name. His sister is still sobbing from fatigue.

I round the corner and still hear crying. I wait for the elevator. I get inside. Even after the doors close I hear crying. If I had seen that beautiful woman any other time and place, I would have thought her too perfect to have miscalculated her journey, too lovely to cradle a crying child.

Some say we only do kind things out of selfishness. We do good deeds to feel better about ourselves and not really to help others.

This is true for me. I am selfish. I helped that woman with her kids, because I recognized myself in her. I've also miscalculated the distance on a walk with my kids. I've also carried a crying child too many miles.

I'm crying and a little sad. I am embarrassed because I'm still learning to accept help when I need it. I don't know how I would have reacted if someone offered me help. I might have said "no."

I'm crying and a little happy. I might have said "yes." The

next time I need help, I will try to accept it. Otherwise, I might miss the chance to walk a mile with a stranger who briefly shares my burden, offers a few words, and then walks away without goodbye.

I DON'T WANT CHRISTMAS

I too recently stood next to my father's grave. I don't want Christmas this year. The glowing lights, the scent of pine, the holiday music mean nothing to me when I'd rather have darkness and silence. I don't want Christmas, because Christmas is happiness.

I am the reason I'm out in the cold. That's the problem with grief. It makes us move away from things that would normally comfort us. I hate grief. While I should be mourning my dad, I'm busy shutting down all my systems. I cannot move. I cannot taste. I cannot feel joy. I have no room for it. The inn is full.

I've been looking for a manger. So many friends and strangers have tried to build a roof over me and my family in our time of grief. They have sent flowers and food and handwritten notes to make you weep. A friend helped my kids to decorate the Christmas tree when I could not touch a single ornament. Even after it was completely done, the tree, the light, the ornaments were foreign to me. How had they made me happy before?

When my daughter was born, I had my nativity story. But this year there are no miracles unless you count tears. Unless you count the flowers and food and handwritten notes. Unless you count the hugs and softly spoken words. Unless you count those who knew when not to hug and just give you a pat on the back and keep walking. Unless you count the miracle of the stranger who embraced me when I unexpectedly cried last week. Grief does not require privacy. I thought it did.

I don't have any shelter from the storm of grief, but I like the rain. The wind has always been a spirit to me. I don't have a manger yet. The inn is full of sadness, but the manger is quiet and clean.

I am looking at Christmas through strange eyes. I love Christmas. I love Christmas carols. I love Christmas cards with the Three Wise Men. And now I know why. They were the miracles that brought food and flowers and handwritten notes. They are friends and strangers who have lifted me up. They reconstructed my bones and my breath.

My great sadness is that my father passed away just before Thanksgiving and Christmas. He did not live to see my first book published. I know he would have liked it. He enjoyed every book he read. I wish I had one more day with him. He read the nativity story to our family on Christmas morning every year of my life. Until this year.

I have not found a way to thank every person who has touched my family during our mourning. I am thankful for those who are wise when I've been weak. I'm thankful for those who have brought Christmas to my house and left it waiting for me at the door. I don't want Christmas, but I'm trying to make room. There is always room for happiness. Even if it has to wait until next year.

Merry Christmas.

IF WE UNDERSTOOD

Children ask questions. Why don't we? Where did the plane go? Why is the skin of my youth not the skin that I have now? Why do we grieve? Why do we claim we know when time begins, when logically time can have no beginning or end?

I'm like a child. I'm full of whys.

When my oldest child turned ten, I was supposed to write her a letter. But I couldn't write to her or any of my children. Some days I think I understand. Other days I'm lost. Instead of writing to my kids, I wrote to my dad. Heaven is a poor word for where he is.

On days when I struggle in life, I try to remember that we understand what we see. Not more or less. When we don't understand, when life is full of mystery, we imagine and create so we can feel at peace.

Life is survival. Life is making sense of mysteries.

If we understood everything, there would be no music. No lyrics or song.

There would be no painting. No chisel on marble. No hands on clay. We would not seek to replicate or refine. We would not look for beauty.

There would be no medicine. Some of us would live to old age and some of us would die too young. Eighty years old is too young to die. I don't understand death or life or any mystery.

There would be no technology. No phones, no airplanes. If we understood that our feet should stay on the ground there would be no reason to fly.

There would be no books.

There would be nothing but us eating and dying. We don't all believe in heaven. We don't all understand. It is a good thing we aren't all the same. Some days I believe every one of us is right in our wrong interpretations of life.

We don't actually like mysteries unless they can be solved. We want to know. We want to understand, but we can't. No one wants to believe that some lost things are never found.

We will find the lost things in our imagination. We will try to understand through art, invention, and music. Stories are born each time we can't find an answer. I will look for lost things in the clouds and in the sea. Eventually I will make up a story, an answer, just right for me.

THE GHOST OF PASCUAL PÉREZ

It's spring time in Atlanta and some are ready for baseball.
I look for ghosts.

I don't remember missing a Braves game until I went to
college. All through my childhood, baseball was our habit.
When we moved to Georgia my mother learned, and then
knew, everything there was to know about the sport.

One of my sisters would sit on the floor in front of the
coffee table. She kept track of the game on a scorecard from
the newspaper. At the end of the game, her grid rivaled any
scientific log. There was my spring and summer and fall. She
had a poster of Dale Murphy in her bedroom. He held a neon
glowing bat. He was a superhero. My other sister had a
baseball signed by Glenn Hubbard. My mother's favorite
player was Chris Chambliss. You would not know about my
family's love of baseball if you met them today. Baseball is
gone from us now.

My father would explain Atlanta driving to out of town
visitors with the story of Pascaul Pérez. Pascual got on I-285
heading for the Braves stadium. He drove for hours and
hours circling the city, not realizing I-285 was a perimeter, a
loop. He drove until he was almost out of gas. When he
stopped at a service station, someone recognized him and
directed him to the stadium. He showed up twenty minutes

late, and another pitcher had already taken the mound. The nickname "I-285" stuck. The highway is still there. But Pascual is gone. He died in his home country, the Dominican Republic, in a botched robbery. I wonder about the moment when history becomes legend.

My dad is gone, too. This is my first baseball season without him, but in all honesty I haven't watched an entire baseball game in years. The night my husband and I got our cat, our first baby, we'd gone to a Braves game with my parents. My cat is eleven years old now, and her name is Greg Maddux. He, the man, pitched a one hit game that night. Good enough reason to memorialize a victory through her, the cat.

When I was a kid, my parents had time to sit with me and my sisters for nine innings and sometimes more. We would take MARTA to the old stadium where I watched football and baseball growing up. The old stadium is now a parking lot. The new stadium will also become the old stadium and soon enough baseball will be gone from the city. If there are too many ghosts in Atlanta it's because we have made them.

Years ago, I saw a ghost as I drove into San Francisco. The 101 merges with the 280 highway at a point slightly elevated over the city. There is a perfect view of the baseball stadium. One morning just as I caught sight of the baseball stadium, I noticed the shadow of my grandfather sitting in the back seat of my car. The sunlight broke through the morning fog, and the outline of a man in a fedora rode with me for a moment. Then he was gone. I wonder what he wanted to say. I felt unsettled, but it made me feel better to go to a baseball game that day.

Driving home from work, I circled I-285 and imagined the ghost of Pascual Pérez was riding with me. These days, he is not lost. He likes the journey. He is good company. He will ride with me whether or not there is baseball in Atlanta. Maybe that famous night as he drove round and round the city for hours, he was talking to a ghost in the backseat of his car. Now the ghost of Pascual Pérez is happy when rush-hour takes three hours. If there is hell, there is heaven. Circling Atlanta for all eternity might be nice, if you believe the baseball stadium is around the next bend.

LETTER TO MY FATHER

Dear Daddy,

Five years ago, I wrote a letter to my children. At the time, I had three children. The oldest was turning five, and I wanted to let them know my wishes and who I was and who I hoped to become. I never hoped to be grieving, but I am. Even though you've been gone three months, I still feel that I can get you back. We want you back with us.

Now I have four children. The baby asks Nana where you are. She is three and will be the likeliest one to forget you. She stands in your empty closet, above her four hangers dangle like stars. If I touch them they make the sound of bells. She wants to know when you are coming back. Nana tells her the truth, but the baby looks skeptical. For her there is no such thing as never. So she continues to wait.

The oldest sometimes stands at my side and hugs me. She looks up at me with sad eyes but a smile on her face. She is not yet 10. She will remember you the best. I wish my kids were older. I wish that they had more of you to remember. The oldest hopes she can heal me with her embrace. That's what I've always taught her so it must be true.

The second one talks about you often. You are in her prayers. She likes to remember you when the rest of us try to forget. "Papa, used to read books with me." If we could pick a legacy for you this would be it.

The boy is like a little man. He mentions nothing. He is like you. He keeps secrets. He did not cry at the funeral or before or after. The night you died he sat outside your bedroom. He did not go in. Maybe he could best sense your presence and your absence. He asked me if I could find pictures of heaven on the computer. I told him no. He paused, "Can you show me pictures of hell?" Again, I told him no. He paused once more, then whispered, "Can you show me pictures of the underworld?" I laughed until my sad tears were gone. I sat outside your bedroom on the floor with him. We looked at pictures of angels and demons and clouds and fire. Maybe he is like you. Maybe he is like me. He wants to see all the possibilities.

Your son-in-law has your winter coat. He put it on one day, and I marveled at how men of different stature could wear the same coat. He looked nice. I envied him. I waited until he left, and then I cried.

Everyone wants to know how mom is doing. We're doing our best to fill the house with kids and noise and mess, but I don't think it takes away Nana's sadness. That's okay. We are learning to love our sadness. I took her shopping, and she stopped in front of the bakery items. Her eyes stared for a long time at one thing, a blueberry tart. "He would have liked this," she said. Her voice went back 48 years and all the days in between. "He would have liked this," she said and bought the blueberry treat because she needed something in the house to make you happy.

I am the same as always. I laugh at inappropriate things. I wrote your obituary. The real one. The funny one. The one they wouldn't send to the newspaper. They weren't ready to laugh. They didn't realize that neither was I.

Thank you for putting shoes on my feet. Thank you for telling me about the time you saw Robert Frost read poetry. Thank you for calling me Sugar and reading with my kids. Thank you and mom for rescuing me every day of my life.

Even though you were an avid reader, we never spoke

about my writing. I wanted to give you a book filled with words I'd written. I'm sorry it took me so long. I hope you can read my book from heaven. It is for you. And mom. And the same with everything else I write. I learned one thing from you, words are important. Even if they are lies. Even if they are fiction.

Daddy, we miss you and we love you. We will see you in the firelight on a cold day. We will find you in the clouds of a blue sky. We will smile, even if we are sad inside.

THE PROBLEM WITH THE TOOTH FAIRY

I never believed in Santa Claus. His handwriting looked too much like my father's. But I wasn't the kid who spoiled Santa for other kids. I loved believing in things. Aliens, Santa Clause, the Falcons going back to the Super Bowl. I believe in magic, but I'm honest about it. It doesn't help that I won't pretend to be the Tooth Fairy.

My daughter lost a tooth and it took me three days to remember to put money under her pillow. By money, I mean a single United States of America one dollar bill. One dollar. Not $5. Not $20. A dollar is great considering I got a quarter at her age, and I'm four times her age now. Simple math. One dollar.

The problem isn't the money. My kids just accept the money gladly. They love the $1, because the alternative is me forgetting indefinitely. I'm the worst Tooth Fairy ever.

My daughter came to me disappointed because the Tooth Fairy forgot to visit her. I reminded my daughter that our Tooth Fairy never visits on the first night. We have a Second Night Tooth Fairy. This didn't seem to bother her. The next morning when there was still no visit from the Tooth Fairy, she began to worry.

I did something terrible. This is what I said.

"Honey, it takes a village to be the Tooth Fairy. Do you

know how many are in the village today? One. Your mother is a village of one. She forgot to put the money under the pillow," I said. Had my husband remembered, he would have pulled out a $5, because he is The Good Tooth Fairy. He remembers. Usually. He pays well. He is cheerful. But he had forgotten too. I looked at my eight year old and said, "There is no Tooth Fairy. And if you want a dollar it might help if you left the Tooth Fairy a note so she'd remember."

It gets worse. So much worse. My daughter pulls out a letter from behind her back. "I did write a note."

Dear Tooth Fairy, I lost my tooth, but I don't want you to take it. Please don't take it.

There in her note was belief and faith and hope in magic. All I could say is, "Check tomorrow morning." I'm a bad and horrible mom. The next morning my daughter found this note from the Tooth Fairy and $1. Guilt does not change the payout.

Thank you for being patient with the Tooth Fairy. I loved the note you wrote and will treasure the tooth, but you can keep it. There is magic in the world even if sometimes grownups forget. It is your job to remind them every day. Have fun without your fangs! Love, the Tooth Fairy.

And here is where the story gets stranger. She gets the note and comes running to me the next morning with her face full of joy. I told my daughter there was no Tooth Fairy. I told her the incompetent human playing the part of the tooth fairy was me, the surly mother.

But all my daughter shouted was, "She remembered!"

For some reason she forgot my honesty and lateness and surly attitude. She didn't need $5 or $20. She is looking for magic. And that's the worst problem about believing in anything or anyone. It's when you look for magic and actually find it.

CAFFEINATED LOVE

Coffee shops are the most depressing and exhilarating places on earth. Anxiety + Adrenaline. There's a particular coffee shop on the West Side of Atlanta that does not brew decaf. I'm a non-coffee drinker who frequents coffee shops. I drink tea and steamed milk. I don't understand your caffeinated love. When I'm feeling wild, I order decaf with lots of sugar and cream.

Then the guy behind the counter tells me they don't brew decaf. I panic.

"I'll have regular," I say while trying to play it cool. I have an hour to kill between two meetings downtown. What's wrong with a little caffeine? Nothing. I'm not against it. I don't like bitter things. I don't like beer or wine or coffee. I have a plan to like all these things when I grow up. But who wants to do that?

I sit at the coffee bar with my regular coffee. I drink it, but they will pay the price. I'm going to write for a little while. I have a yellow legal pad and a pen from a different coffee shop, one from my side of town. The side of town that likes to name its coffee shops after animals. The side of town that brews decaf. I feel very far from home.

After about three sips, I realize this regular coffee from a coffee shop that doesn't make decaf is super-charged. My heart starts racing, and my eyes fill with tears. I can clearly read the tattoo under the plaid shirt of the barista. It's two lines of poetry. The molecules of caffeine fuse into my blood. I look to the left and can see the future. Time gets unbearably slow. I stand up and do a bit of an Irish jig in the center of the coffee shop. The caffeination is total and complete.

No one notices me because they are used to the caffeine rush. They sit and gaze or crazy talk through the malaise of panic and work avoidance. No one goes to a coffee shop to work. They go to see people. They go to shake the quiet from their brain.

My brain has run away, and I peer into my cup.

"What's in this?" I ask the guy behind the bar. He doesn't answer. You know him. He's actually a really nice guy. He laughs and tells me he has a new motorcycle. We go outside to look at his Harley. This is the honest truth. I am stone cold drunk on coffee at 11 a.m. I want to jump on the bike and take a ride, but I stopped drinking the coffee after the third sip and my judgment is returning. Me on a motorcycle would have made a nice selfie.

The caffeine buzz is so bad my hands are shaking. My heart isn't even beating anymore. I'm one continuous buzz of vibration.

"This is crazy," I say. I'm too old and mom-ish to be talking to tattooed boys on motorcycles. Caffeine, it seems, lowers my inhibitions. I go back inside and hand-write 500 words on a single sheet of legal paper. Caffeine, it seems, increases my output. Which would be wonderful, except that the words I wrote are the ones you see on this page. No Pulitzer Prize winning novel here. Caffeine is selfish in its intoxication.

Let me enjoy my steamed milk. I don't need to have coffee. It works too well, and seeing the future once is enough for me. Besides, I like the quiet in my brain.

FORGETTING

I say "no" to birthday parties and playdates, because chances are good that I won't remember to show up. I forget things all the time. I have good excuses. I'm socially awkward. I'm anti-social. I have four kids, and on any given weekend we have two or three birthday party invites. But these are just excuses. Now I own up to my lapses in memory. I admit the real reason I say "no" is because I forget.

A year ago, I received a text message from a friend.

"Sorry you missed the party last night," she wrote.

"What party?" I responded.

There was a long gap until she sent another message.

"My wedding," she wrote.

We'd had lunch dates at the Brickstore to discuss her plans. The event happened around the corner from where I live. The DJ was a man I'd first seen at another friend's wedding. The save the date card was on my dresser. It was the couple kissing at Disney World. There were a dozen reasons why I should have remembered, but I didn't. I should have been there, but I had forgotten. I didn't have another engagement or a problem finding a babysitter. No one got sick. Nothing prevented me from attending the wedding but me.

Forgetting meant two terrible things. One, it suggested I

didn't value our friendship. Two, it meant that my mind could not be trusted.

I have another friend who drove hours to take her daughter to camp only to find out that camp started the next day. I could imagine that happening to me. I hear story after story about people forgetting life. Maybe disproportionately it is parents, but it is all of us.

We are overworked. We are over-stimulated. We are tired. You would think I'd gotten better since the missed wedding.

One weekend, I arrived at a birthday party venue only to discover the event was the day before. My three-year old was wearing her pinkest dress. The one with a tu-tu skirt. It was her first birthday party. She talked about it all week. And I could only think to console her by walking her over to the adjacent grocery store to buy a cupcake. Instead she asked for a cucumber.

Back at home, I washed and sliced the cucumber. I watched her eat, and I envied her mind. She has things on her side like youth and no responsibilities. Grown-ups are busy. Work does not end at 5 pm or on Friday anymore. When people say TGIF, I wonder why. I still have a weekend full of more work to do. Grown-ups have distraction. After all, our phones are not just phones, but camera and video camera, video games, TV and movies. Computer and telegraph and radio.

Being busy and distracted are terrible reasons to forget.

I sat in my car thinking. I was all alone and parked in my garage. Even in the relative shade and safety, it grew hot. I have a mini-van with four car seats. They were so empty. I could barely see them in the rearview mirror. I was trying to see behind me. I was trying to gauge my mind and the past. I tried to remember the things I had a habit of forgetting.

When my father died, I sat in the funeral home with my mother and sisters. The funeral director peppered us with questions.

"What was his social security number?"

My mother said the number without glancing at any

papers or anyone in the room. After a few more questions, the man asked, "How long were you married?"

My mother paused. She looked at me and my sisters.

"What year did you get married?" the man asked again. My mother had no answer.

My sisters and I started to calculate. "Forty-seven years." They'd been married 47 years and my mother had forgotten. We blamed it on grief and shock and the rush of questions.

Maybe forgetting has a little to do with being busy or distracted. Maybe forgetting is a paralysis of our mind when we are stressed. Maybe it is a bigger danger than we think. I am more afraid of forgetting than I am of other dangerous things.

All through the funeral and the weeks after my father's death, people would repeat this comment about my then two-year-old. "She will be the one to forget him. She will never remember her grandfather." My 16-year-old niece was lucky, they would say. She was sadder, but she would have memories of her Papa. Forgetting was worse.

There are so many reasons why people cry when someone dies. I finally understand that grief this week. I thought it was about the absence. I thought it was the selfish wish for one more day. But our tears are because we fear forgetting those we love. And we fear being forgotten.

THE VIEW FROM SPAIN

One weekend, I found myself in Madrid. It was my first trip to Spain, and I was terribly excited. Every once in a while, in my very ordinary life, extraordinary things happen. Extraordinary things like a trip to Spain to celebrate my best friend's 40th birthday.

She is obsessed with soccer, football or fútbol. Her favorite team is in Real Madrid. While we were in college, I was the one who tortured her with football and baseball and soccer games. I was the one who knew the rules and enjoyed entire Saturdays in a stadium. Now she is the person I used to be. She briefed me on the players and their injuries and personal dramas.

Two friends. Forty years. Four days in Madrid. And fútbol.

We spent all weekend talking like we are teenagers again. Twenty years of friendship. So many years that feel like yesterday.

I knew that as a traveler, I should be quiet and respectful and reverent and adventurous. But the people in Spain could tell immediately that I was from America. My husband says it's because I smile too much. Smiling is a cultural thing. Have you ever seen a caricature of Jimmy Carter or Bill Clinton? Southerners are smiling people. I can't help it. I don't like to

41

hug, but I will knock your socks off with my smile.

In the taxi from the airport, the driver asked where I was from.

"Atlanta," I said.

"Oh. Atlanta, Georgia," he said.

The way he said Georgia was amazing. We say "Geor-Ja," but he said "Gee-Or- Gia."

"Yes," I said. We both started smiling.

Much to my disappointment, Spain did not feel foreign or exotic. It felt like home. It was busy like New York, vibrant like San Francisco. The people were friendly identical to my life in Atlanta. Atlanta, Georgia.

We enjoyed octopus, pulpo. We walked all day and night. We got lost in artwork, abstract and real. My truly American moment happened when I fell in love with a picture of a small dog. I stepped closer to see the title, "The Drowning Dog." I decided the dog was just swimming. The artist Francisco de Goya likes things both beautiful and shadowy. That's the way I see the world.

I felt myself falling in love with Spain.

On game day, the security guards checked the other fans, but not us. Not the Americans. No chance of us hurling broken bottles onto the field. Or maybe it was our smiles. We smiled when we approached the stadium. We smiled when we took our seats. I waited for a moment when things felt foreign. I waited to find a sight or flavor or aroma that was new to me. But that moment never came. Spain was different, but not unfamiliar.

People continued to ask me where I was from. Everyone said, "Atlanta, Georgia!" in response and smiled. We were the same.

The cheers of the football match erupted around me. What's not to love about a little fútbol? The world feels small and good when you are cheering with strangers and friends. We watched and jumped up in excitement. Then suddenly a little disappointment. Followed by an unexpected goal and joy again.

I could see the whole world from Spain. I could see my house across the globe. I thought of it as shadowy and beautiful. I knew I could make a home anywhere I found smiling faces. I was at home as we enjoyed the game. I felt just a bit Spanish. It felt like another day in my ordinary life.

MY MAGICAL INSIDES

I don't care about left or right. It's all nonsense. All I ask of you is this. Be kind. Be decent. And don't be greedy. —Nickolas Butler, "Shotgun Lovesongs"

I don't engage in political discussions. If you start one with me, I'll turn the conversation to *Star Trek*. In the future, I hope we'll be civil in our discourse. But I know people will always argue and disagree. Still, I dream of the day when there will be equality for all people, for all women. These days, having a uterus is a dangerous thing, but for me it is magic.

When you're a girl, as soon as you turn 12 years old, people start talking about your insides. You get your period and suddenly you are magic. You are Eve with the apple. Girls are either objectified or scorned. Boys don't have this trouble. When you're a 12-year-old boy, the world leaves you alone. Boys get to be kids as long as they can.

After little girls become women, people want to know what happens next. Are you going to have sex or abstain? Are you going to get married? Are you using contraceptives? Are you going to have babies? Did you mean to get pregnant or was it an accident? By goodness, you've got all that magic locked up inside of you. And it is hidden magic. How are you going to use it? It is power. It is mystery. The world needs to

44

understand your magic. Worst of all, the world feels compelled to tell you what to do with it.

If you watched *Star Trek*, you know that Uhura (in The Original Series) had a great career. She had no boyfriend or husband. She had no kids. She was smart and adventurous. She had curves and showed her legs. She had magic. She was thoughtful. Nobody judged her for the things she had or the things she didn't have. Nothing seemed to be missing in her life.

Real life women, with magical insides, are judged by everything. From when we get our cycle to how we decide to use it. Having sex is wrong. Not having sex is weird. Enjoying sex is very wrong. Having a baby is conforming to a paternalistic society. Not having a baby is selfish. Being unable to conceive is a disappointment. Adopting is suspicious. We women with magical insides cannot make any choice without it being the wrong one.

Some days I'd rather live in outer space.

What does the world need to know about boys? Zilch. Obviously, boys ARE having sex. They are men. They don't have magic. All of their parts are on the outside. There is no mystery or responsibility. No one asks how, why, or what they are doing to protect themselves. This double standard doesn't even make me mad. I have a son. He is great, but he isn't magical. The world makes assumptions about him that this evil mother is going to correct. All those questions asked of my daughters will be asked of him.

I will not talk politics with you. I will not debate religion with you. But I will get upset at the suggestion that women make decisions flippantly. We deliberate about every choice we make. We ingest hormones that alter our bodies and minds. We have children, and suddenly we heighten our awareness of the disappointments in the world. Single? Child-free? We live under never ending scrutiny.

Here is my politics: "Women are not thoughtless." That is all. Not right or left. Women do not need to be unified in their choices, because we are not unified in our experiences.

My decisions in life would be horrifically, tragically wrong for another woman.

Some people react to injustice by boycotting corporations. I should boycotted everything. I don't. I should have boycotted craft stores and low cost retails stores and fast food chains. I should have boycotted stores I've never entered and stores that entice into spending too much money. Instead I sharpened my voice, and I thought about the future. I thought about *Star Trek*.

Conversations about reproductive habits and reproductive rights make me uncomfortable. Would I have liked Uhura better if she had a boyfriend or babies? Probably not. Maybe I liked her because she was not always defined by her race and gender. Maybe I liked her because her magic, her female power, could not be disguised.

You can't control my amazing uterus and lady bits and girly parts. My magical insides drive people to debate, boycott, and vote. But I have another astonishing woman place. It is called a brain. Your politics might be different if you realized we were really arguing about my mind.

Instead of asking me about politics, ask me about my favorite episode of *Star Trek*. That's the best way to find out what I really think.

MILF AM I

We should talk to our kids about sex. We should talk to ourselves about sex every year we further settle into our skin.

Men like me. I used to think this was because of my knowledge of baseball and my love of *Star Trek*. But it's really my "I don't give a rat's ass" attitude. I don't rise to the bait. I don't demure. I don't take to heart all the silliness in the world that is someone else's insecurities. Most of all, I don't take any of it seriously. Maybe that will change one day. I'm not 42 yet.

I get hit on in the strangest places. One day, I took my visiting in-laws on a walk through Little Five Points. I pushed a stroller with my oldest child inside. A man called out to me.

"Can I get your number?" he asked. He was a normal looking guy, not indigent or insane.

"These are my in-laws. I probably shouldn't give you my number," I answered.

He looked at my mother and father-in-law. He looked at the baby in the stroller. "Your husband won't mind," he said. I declined again. He told me I had a pretty smile and walked away.

Another day I was shopping in Whole Foods, and a young man stood next to me. He was a white hipster dude. I could tell he was watching me despite my four kids running wild around my shopping cart.

"Have you tried the turkey meatloaf?" He asked. Best pickup line ever. I had tried the turkey meatloaf. It is my favorite.

"Can I call you sometime?" he asked.

I looked at the kids and then him. "I have my hands full as it is," I told him. That was the truth. I can't really handle four kids and a job and a writing career and a husband AND a boyfriend. Really? What would the cat think?

I'm not pretty by the conventional standards. With makeup, I look nice. Without makeup I look like Michael Jackson in the "Thriller" video. I've got kids and a grumpy attitude. My weight and physical health could be improved. I've got both the muffin top and bottom.

And I still have it going on.

I'm looking forward to birthdays like 40 and 42. I hear retirement homes are hot beds of hedonism. All that free time and hot sex, followed by an ice cream social at 3 p.m. Sign. Me. Up. Why would I worry about 42 when I've got big plans for 82?

I don't think anyone gets into bed and says, "I'm going to have 39 year-old-style sex tonight." That would be a little Depeche Mode mixed with New Edition twirled with Silver Spoons and a splash of Facts of Life (before the George Clooney episodes).

Do you know how much sex you have at 20 years old? Zero. Do you know how much sex you have at 42? A lot more than zero. Then I wondered if it was a race or cultural thing. Maybe men of a certain race and demographic just think about sex instead of having it.

In the meantime, I'm waiting to stop being so sexy. My children and in-laws are not enough of a buffer to scare off potential suitors.

I went to a writing group where the other attendees were all child-free and twenty-something. As we were leaving, one of the men asked me how it was being a mother and a writer.

"I'm a proud soccer mom. I don't let my kids stop me

from writing or being MILFy."

The expression on this kid's face was priceless. He was shocked. I think he wanted me to talk about balance or discipline or Maya Angelou or Margaret Atwood or Chaucer or Dickens. After that, he only ever asked me about my writing.

I actually caused a little incident at the car wash on Ponce another day. This time, I was wearing make-up and a red dress and had every bit of my work day A-game on. I forgot to not bring my A-game to the car wash. These jokers were fighting to detail my car. The mini-van with the granola bar wrappers and cereal crumbs and four car seats. The men didn't care.

That's how sexy my car is. That's how sexy my life is. And turning 42 isn't going to change that.

THE BROKEN BOOKSHELF

I'm the Pied Piper of books. I buy books, I win books, and books are given to me. Books find me. At night our books multiply. In the morning, we give books away. I match people with books. I've called myself a book whisperer. If you tell me a few things about yourself, I can suggest a book for you. Any genre.

I want to teach my kids that reading any kind book is okay. One of them likes to read below her reading level. At first I agonized over this. Why wasn't she reading *War and Peace* at 10 years old? Another likes books with pictures. That's not reading! But then I realized that looking at pictures and flipping pages is as good as reading. Never mind that he is six years old.

Our summer project is stocking the little free libraries around town. At first, my kids were embarrassed at the idea. "Mommy, I don't think you should be touching that." "Mommy, if we take a book and not leave a book isn't that stealing?" "Mommy, can we just go to the park already?"

But after our first book drop, as we walked toward the park, my kids noticed a couple looking in the little library we just filled. A woman and man each took a book we'd just left in the library. My eight year old, the most suspicious, started jumping up and down. "They took a book!"

"That, my dear, is the point." Now my kids like checking-up on the little libraries. The one by City Hall has the fastest turnover. We see it empty, and by the time we come back, it is already filled up again. Often we just tidy the books and stare at the reading options. We wonder what books people have read, what they want to share, what might someone read. This fills us with great happiness.

Each book isn't just a story. It is an entire life. A life can be saved or healed or changed by a book. Books are not for the elite or educated. This is where the story changes. This isn't really a happy story. The bookshelf is broken.

We went to the little library in front of Clairemont Elementary School, and it was empty. Not a book inside. I'd been watching this library for some time. It was always empty. No turnover at all. This is the little library that started our crusade. A person built this beautiful structure by hand and no one thought to add books. How come people accepted the little empty library? We brought books and filled it up, but something was wrong.

I recently spoke at the Atlanta-Fulton County Library. Before I went, people joked with me about the number of homeless people I might encounter during my talk. Bookish people, regular people who love books would rather be at coffee shops and bookstores. Big city public libraries are shunned.

My son got to meet the author and illustrator of the *Fancy Nancy* series and someone commented to me that I should have brought my daughters. I got a little mad. My son doesn't particularly like *Fancy Nancy*, but he likes this book, and [drumroll], he is reading the words in the book. For me, that makes a good book.

I find myself around bookish people. This used to bring me a lot of joy, but these days bookish people irritate me. They are no fun. They don't care about everyone reading. They only care about "smart" people reading "good" books. Writers are developing a bad habit of condescending, marginalizing, and creating an invisible class system.

Everyone deserves to share the bookshelf.

No one can ever control you if you read.

Reading a book can improve your creativity in cooking and art and music and building little free libraries.

If someone tells you shouldn't read a specific book or a specific kind of book, you should read everything.

Read in the closet or under the covers with a flashlight. Read like women and slaves were once denied this privilege. Read like it might be denied you one day.

Every kind of person should read regardless of money and education.

Every book has value. The pink fancy books. The books with only pictures. Bad books. Sexy books. Even the used and used and used again books are worth something.

I have author friends and teachers dropping off books at my house. We are spending the summer filing up the shelves and hoping someone who needs a book finds a book. Books find me. I'm thankful every day, because books love me. The bookshelf might be broken, but it can be fixed. You can fix it. I know this because we haven't written the ending yet.

THE UNMADE BED

How do you keep something clean? You don't care if it gets dirty.
I recently took a picture of my three-year-old in an ivory color knit dress. It was a momentous occasion because it's a dress all three of my girls have worn. There are seven years, and a brother, between these little ladies. Keeping anything that long or that clean takes skill. The dress looks brand new.

A friend asked me how I keep things clean. That's funny, because my life is a mess. She was focused on the ivory dress and my wild child crawling around on the daycare floor.

"I don't care if it gets dirty," I told her. This is true. My kids wear Easter dresses on any random day of the week. We go to the park as often in jeans as we do in sequins. Nothing is sacred. We don't control the chaos and the dirt anymore.

I grew up in a very clean house. My parents made their bed every day. Each morning, my mom would grab one end of the sheet and my dad the other. They tucked in the sheet and pulled up the covers. They'd use their hands like irons to flatten everything into its proper place. If one parent or the other was absent, the bed was still made. Every day.

I didn't make my bed as a kid or a teen, but I made it in college. There was no room for an unmade bed. A little chaos took up a lot of space. I kept that habit into my early adulthood. I kept that apartment in Redwood City, California really clean. I kept that apartment in Buckhead spotless. I'm the person who likes hotel bed sheets tucked in tightly. I like to sleep perfectly swaddled.

I've been told it is important to make your bed every day. This habit will endow me with qualities like a sense of accomplishment and order and stability. I like a made bed. The memory of my parents making their bed is one of my happiest memories of them. They were thoughtful in how they raised me. The bed was not a symbol of perfection, but perseverance. I love that.

I start the night in order, but when I wake there is disorder. Sometimes I keep my bed unmade, and I like that too.

I don't sleep well. I don't sit still. I have to learn to slow down. Since I became a mother, since my dad died, I some days crawl into my unmade bed for five minutes of quiet. I wouldn't dare crawl in a made bed until bedtime. The unmade bed invites me back at odd hours.

There are virtues in an unmade bed.

I find children in my bed. During the day, they climb in with a book or a baby doll. One morning, I woke up and realized I slept all night on a LEGO.

I begin and end my day in the same tangled, swirling mess. I like tucking and swaddling myself in only to be unbound by morning.

I might stop in the middle of a terrible stressful moment and collapse in the bed. It is a bed where I can stop and breathe and cry.

A made bed, a spread bed, is a device. Like a can opener or a chair. It has a purpose. An unmade bed is a nest. I have stopped for a five minute cry, climbed into my bed and instead of crying, found myself smiling. The sheet is twisted to one side, I am underneath double the blankets. Life becomes funny and insignificant. I am smiling in my unmade bed.

My bed is made some days, but not all. I asked my sisters, the two who witnessed the ritual of my parents. One always makes her bed. The other never. I'm the one in between. I don't care if it is made or not. I don't mind if the ivory dress gets dirty. I don't care if my kids climb trees dressed in sequins.

I'd rather the virtue of crying or smiling over the sense of accomplishment. I might not accomplish anything in this life anyway.

GO THE F*K BACK TO SCHOOL

Dear Teachers, you may ask my kids what they did this summer. I'm not sure what they will say, but I'll tell you the truth.

To some, we wasted our summer. I did not send my kids to sleep away camp. They can sleep away when they get to college. They have had their fill of sports and art and music camps. My kids wanted to stay at home. They wanted to stay at Nana's house. They wanted to play with their cousins. They asked to do nothing.

We don't know how to do nothing. And yet nothing is my favorite thing. Doing nothing is a long lost friend. I spent my childhood summers doing nothing. I never went to day camp or sleep away camp. My afternoons were alone doing nothing. I grew up in a lot of quiet and boredom.

As soon as this summer started, my kids missed school. They wanted the learning and the structure. I thought I could replicate this. I thought mommy-summer-camp-of-nothing was a great idea. Here is what happened and why they need to go back the f*k to school.

They ate sliced watermelon off of Christmas plates. They watched every episode of *Justice League* on Netflix. We filled the little free libraries with books. We prowled the streets for art on a "Free Art Friday Atlanta" #fafatl scavenger hunt. We got care packages from Taiwan and Bosnia. We met author Chris Colfer. We paraded on July 4th and waved American flags. Without my help, they made silly putty. Seriously.

We dance partied to my favorite songs from my college days and discovered most are inappropriate for kids. One of my kids is rhythmless. One has a little too much rhythm for my comfort. We watched young Michael Jackson and the Jackson 5ive sing "ABC," a good song when you are missing school. We watched older Michael Jackson sing, and they still danced. We had dance party to new songs. I panicked when I heard the lyrics, "Trash the hotel . . . Let's get drunk on the mini bar." My kids needed the guidance of a real music teacher.

The cousins taught them to play poker with poker chips. Kids playing poker is a lot like that painting of dogs playing poker, but with more crying. It turned out that the teen cousins don't know how to play poker, either.

They read more this summer than other summers. Just at the point when TV and nothingness has thoroughly fried your brain, a book becomes a delicious retreat.

We went to every park. We went to Fernbank 20 gazillion times. They were too scared to see the shark IMAX movie, but then spent hours sitting in a replica of a whale heart. That's scary. Ask Jonah.

Security busted us at the High Museum of Art for unauthorized use of our sketch books. Then we got the badge with official artist passes so we could continue to steal creativity from other creative canvases.

We went to the pool. We contemplated the burning pain of sunscreen on your face and the burning pain of too much sun. We enjoyed a few naps induced by sun and chlorine and sand and saltwater. We went to the beach without our boogie boards even though we used the boogie boards on snow days.

I made them watch old *Star Trek* and newer *Star Trek*. The kids developed serious concerns about the state of Starfleet and Ferengi affairs. Maybe I was doing this summer thing right.

I love snow days, and I love summer. We don't want summer to end, but we missed learning after the chaos of nothing. I heard the voices of my kids' teachers all summer. "Do you know what Miss so-and-so says about tornados?" "Do you know what Mister what's-his-name told us about the Piedmont Region?" All year we long for summer. Then summer arrives, and we long for school. Now our longing is over.

I hope you enjoyed your summer. But my kids need to go back to school. They need to go the f*k to school. I've never seen so much laundry and dirty dishes and garbage and happiness in my entire life. Kids are funny. They observe. They reflect. Don't forget your sunglasses these first few weeks of school. If you look deep into their eyes you will still see the sunshine of summer.

WHITENING BLACKENING

I could save the city of Decatur time and money. Each year they can ask me, "Is Decatur getting whiter?" and I will say, "Yes." Signs of the whitening are noticeable. I see them everywhere.

The first sign is a doggy bubble window built into the wooden privacy fences so their dogs and small toddlers peek out into the world behind the safety of plexiglass.

I am contributing to the whitening of Decatur. It's not because I dance like Carlton and know all the words (grudgingly) to "Sweet Home Alabama." It's because sometimes the people in Decatur need lessons on being white, and I can help them. One of my neighbors has just one dog. The white rule is two dogs or a dog and a baby. If you only have one dog or one kid I don't know that you are white. White people can have any number of cats. I'm a cat person myself. My cat Greg Maddux equally dislikes everyone regardless of race.

My family was responsible for the blackening of Stone Mountain in the early 80s. I know all about white flight. I saw it. I lived it. It is infinitely more offensive than gentrification. White flight is scarier, too. It's like Hitchcock has written the script. One morning you wake up and all the white people are gone. Shopping centers and homes become vacant overnight.

I like a good zombie story as much as the next person, but white people running away is a bit extreme.

There were precisely two black families in my neighborhood growing up. We were dangerous and disreputable. College-educated parents, nice lawns, kids who were in the band and played soccer. Of the six kids who suffered the white years in Stone Mountains, two went to MIT, two went to Ivy League schools, and one graduated with an engineering degree from Georgia Tech. Me, the black sheep from the black families? I ran off to college in California. That's where I really learned about whiteness. There aren't even black people working at the airport in San Francisco.

The blackening of Stone Mountain was a good thing for me. No one likes to be the only one. It sucks. My friends before high school were: the one Indian kid (now a doctor in DC), the one Korean kid (owns a boutique in Athens), and the white kid with buck-teeth and glasses who dumped me as a friend as soon as we got to high school and her teeth got straightened (I don't know where she is now).

There was no hope of a boyfriend. There is angst of not having any boys like you. There is another type of angst when a boy liked you, called you, visited your house regularly, ate dinner with your family, but you knew he would never ever ask you to the school dance. Because you are black.

I welcomed the blackening.

Eventually there were enough black girls that people became friends with me because they liked me and not because we were all leftovers. I welcomed the black boys with awkward confidence and cologne and the courage to ask me out even if I only talked about *Star Trek*.

I wonder what will happen to my brown kids in whitening Decatur. I would not wish being the only one on anyone. I notice the white moms who don't talk to the black moms. Maybe they'll talk to me. "You're not really black," they say. I make note of the parents who assume that I'm a daycare employee when I pick up my kid from school. I have mastered the art of the pregnant pause. I've had four kids. I can do a wonderful pregnant pause. I wait and wait, and then I smile and say, "I'm just here to pick up my daughter." (And no, I'm not the nanny.)

Some will argue economics with me. It's a socio-economic issue. It's about the class system. I disagree. You aren't looking at me and seeing my paycheck or degree. You are looking at my hair. You are looking at my skin. That's cool, because I'm used to the stares. I'm staring back at you. I admit that I am here for the schools and access to the MARTA line. I'm also here because every so often I walk into my favorite restaurant or coffee house and someone calls me by name. I'm not here for the whiteness or blackness or refusal to acknowledge the other types of people in Decatur.

I have a friend from Maine who I met in college. She could recall being on a road trip with her family and the very first time she saw a black person. That's how white her town was growing up. She had to leave her hometown to find black people. Now that's white. I don't think Decatur will ever get that white. At least not on my watch.

GOOD COP, BAD COP

My dad was the good cop. My mother was the bad cop. She created the laws and the discipline and standards in our house. My dad was the chatty one. My mom was quiet. Being the bad cop meant she was the good parent.

The news is filled with bad cops and bad people. I don't read the news. I don't watch the news. I don't listen to the news. I only read the headlines.

I don't want to be afraid of cops. I don't want to compartmentalize everything into good and bad when we are sometimes both.

I've only ever had one unhappy experience with the police. I was at the movies with a friend when I was a teenager, and our car battery died. The parking lot quickly emptied. Soon we were the only car left. A squad car circled by, and we asked for help. The officer said he couldn't help us and drove off. It was dark, and I was scared. I was such a good kid, that I didn't have a curfew.

My mom, the bad cop, knew I would be home on time. If I was late she would be worried, not angry. We didn't have mobile phones in those days. My friend and I walked until we found a pay phone down the street.

Maybe my race or the police officer's race or what town we lived in matters to some people. Maybe I should have been jaded, but I wasn't. I was disappointed in him, not his uniform.

In the years since, I've witnessed amazing acts of kindness by police officers. The one who changed the car tire for my mom and dad. The ones who showed up when the burglar alarm went off. The one who told me I could do a better job of literally stopping at that stop sign.

I have a friend who is a police officer. I did not know this on first meeting. I found out this detail months later. My first thought was about my past behavior. Had I cursed? Had I disparaged speed traps? I felt inadequate and impressed and glad to know a good cop.

I watch *The Walking Dead.* When the zombie apocalypse hits, having a cop (good or bad) on your team is not a bad idea.

Bad people are guilty of acting without thinking. I try to rationalize the bad news by telling myself that it is news because there is less of bad in the world. Bad is unique and fascinating. We can't report all the good in the world, because there is too much of it.

One of the headlines I read last night made me stop. I wanted to cry. This is why so many people are happy to dump ice water over their heads. We are looking for good. We are willing to create it.

PUTTING ON MY CAPE

My first and last TV appearance occurred when I was four years old. Mister Rogers was filming a special about superheroes, and he interviewed Lou Ferrigno and Bill Bixby about the TV show, *The Incredible Hulk*. The film crew recorded the kids' playground antics at my daycare. We were the superhero generation. My 15 seconds of fame happened as I ran around with my hooded sweatshirt for a cape. A boy pushed me down, but I popped up right away, undaunted.

My first hero was Wonder Woman. The day we left Connecticut bound for Georgia, Wonder Woman was on my chest. It was a pale blue shirt with a glossy iron-on of red, gold, and royal blue. She was a pilot, a leader, and a seeker of truth. I never stopped wanting to be those things I thought I could be at age four.

By the time I got to junior high, there was a poster of Spider-Man on my wall. My sisters regularly bought me comics. I remember the first time I saw Storm. She was earth and wind, without the fire. But she had friends who could blaze.

Even though I am grown, I enjoy the days before Labor Day and the chance to put on my cape again. When Dragon Con comes to town, Atlanta does not just become hot, it becomes super. A couple of years ago, I had my second chance to be on TV. A documentary filmmaker stopped me and asked why I had my kids at Dragon Con.

I didn't tell him the truth.

I told him that it was good for them and their creativity. Maybe that was part of the truth, but it was still more lie than truth. We'd been having a tough year. There are things in life outside our control that bring us down, and not suddenly down, but just piece by piece slower and sadder. One day my second daughter asked me why I decided to be a mom.

"It looks like a lot of hard work," she said, eyeing the dishes, the laundry, the stacks of unopened mail, and the shoes on the floor. "Being a grown-up doesn't seem fun," she added.

I may be the world's worst Tooth Fairy, but I do periodically know how to have fun.

"Being an adult is hard work, but when you grow up you can do anything you want. First you work. Then you play." And I hatched a plan to take them downtown to Dragon Con. The baby was nine months old. The older kids were unsure of the MARTA ride and the costumed figures haunting the train. They weren't sure if we should ask to take pictures with the storm troopers, but we did anyway.

Why has Valentine's Day and Halloween and birthdays and everything turned into a holiday for kids with nothing left for the adults? I love Dragon Con. I love the smiles and hugs and sweaty embraces from strangers.

"Those adults," I said as we walked away from the storm troopers, "they are having fun."

I am not Superwoman. I will never have it all. I will never want it all. I have enough, but some days I really need all my superpowers. I get pushed down. I put on my cape and stand up again. I can still run in bionic slow motion. I know now that being amazing or incredible only means you have more villains to defeat.

Some days you have to put on a costume and save the world. My kids like getting dressed up now. As we left Atlanta on Friday evening a mom dressed as Wonder Woman waved to us in the MARTA station. She was fully costumed in her super heroine swimsuit with cape. Her daughter was Batgirl. I had one of those too. She rushed our way, and we took a picture. Strangers feeling super. Oh, man, we were smiling. We all know how to have fun.

Maybe it is my imagination, but I swear my kids (and all those adults downtown in costumes) act better on the days they put on a cape. This year we adopted a new motto: The only way to become super is to act super. This isn't advice for my kids. It's advice for me. Let's see if it works.

ABOUT SEX

I need to talk to my kids about sex one day soon, before they read about it in a book or see it in a music video. I've been avoiding the subject, and I need to study up on it.

When I was a kid my mother handed me a book about my body and puberty. It was a book about a girl's body. It wasn't a book about a boy's body or my body and another person's body. The puberty book didn't explain sex.

We learned a little about sex at school. They sent us to the old Fernbank Science Center in fourth and sixth grade for Sex Education. I grew up in the scared straight sex generation. I learned that my body does these weird things. Then I learned that the body of the opposite sex does even weirder things. Two people having sex equals getting a disease. If you don't get a disease, you will definitely get pregnant. They showed you the miracle video of a baby being born that will scar you for life.

I actually learned about normal sex from fiction. I read romance novels. Sure the men had swords for man parts and ladies had flower petals for lady parts. That all made sense to me. Those books weren't about sex. They were about love and the ramifications of sex. That's what you learn in fiction.

It used to be: No sex until you are married. But I think this is better: No sex until you have a M.D. or you've voted in two presidential elections. Or better yet: No sex until you are fluent in Middle English.

Have you read "The Canterbury Tales?" Chaucer knew a lot about sex.

Things are different now. If I really have to talk to my kids about sex, it will be about how boys might end up in jail and permanently listed as a sex offenders for having sex, even if they are caught having consensual sex with their girlfriends.

I will talk about the emotions of sex. No matter how equal we think we are, one person in a relationship will inevitably attribute more meaning to sex than the other person. Someone will be hurt. Maybe this situation is best illustrated in fiction. A textbook can't show this. What kind of diagram would I draw to show a broken heart?

I buy my nieces all kinds of books for young adults. Some of them have been banned. Some from authors who like to push the envelope. Kids are smart, but not wise. We've got to be both as adults. We need to be honest about sex. We need to remember what we were like at that age.

I knew I could ask my mom anything. And I did ask her everything. Poor her. Lucky me. I hope my nieces and nephews and my kids understand that I'd rather talk to them about *Star Trek*, but I will talk to them about sex when I need to. I'm not one to be controversial or overt. I know the difference between what's said to shock and what's said to start a conversation. I know what's funny because it's embarrassing and what's funny because it is the truth.

Hopefully, they will ask me any and everything. Yes, I am panicking. Yes, I am a prude. Yes, the worst word I'm prepared to type or say is "nipple." But I am not afraid of the truth. My poor kids. Lucky me. They will find out what I know when they ask me.

MY DAD AND ROBERT FROST

My first nickname was Nikki Giovanni. A family friend, a boy in college, called me Nikki Giovanni from before I can remember. That should be enough to explain why I like the poetry of words and books and writing, except I didn't know who Nikki Giovanni was when I was small. Her name was like a nursery rhyme. I didn't know that she was a real person.

In elementary school, my teacher lined the classroom with photos of famous African-Americans for Black History Month. That was the first time I saw beautiful Nikki, my namesake. It was the first time I knew she was a poet. It was the first time I knew she was real.

Around the same time, I learned about Robert Frost. When my dad saw me reading poetry, he mentioned that he'd seen Robert Frost speak at his college.

My father attended Rutgers University as an international student before desegregation in the United States. African-Americans were not allowed to attend white universities, but black people from other countries could. I should have asked my father more about those years, but I didn't. I should have asked him about the hardships, but my father was a glass half-full kind of man. He never had hardships. I did ask him about Robert Frost.

"What was Robert Frost doing at your school? Why did

you go? Did you like poetry?" I asked. My dad liked books and spy novels and adventure stories. He liked numbers. He was an accountant and a brilliant man. But I never knew him to like poetry.

My dad said, "It was a very big deal. He knew the President. Everyone dressed up. We wore our best suits. The auditorium was full of people."

"How was it? What did he sound like?" I asked. I wanted details.

My father only said, "It was very nice."

I don't think that "nice" qualifies as details, but it was enough to pique my interest. My dad saw Robert Frost with his own eyes. How many people could say this?

My mother took me to Waldenbooks at Northlake Mall where I bought *The Collected Poems of Robert Frost*. I took the poems with me to Lake Alatoona that summer. We would stay in a cabin and spend a decadent week doing nothing. Our days were filled with choices like lake or pool or ping-pong or books. I lounged by the pool with Robert Frost.

Robert Frost was long dead and very far from Georgia and the shores of that manmade lake. Still, I felt close to him. Maybe he was a mythical creature. Writing is a magical thing that might bring people together who may never meet. I would read poetry and try to untangle some meaning in my kid life. I decided to try being a writer when I was a kid. I promised myself that if I could ever see a famous writer, I would. And I would remember the details.

Rita Dove wore brightly colored nail polish. She embraced me, and welcomed my shy silence when I could not think of any proper questions to ask her.

Pat Conroy's hands were softer than any I'd ever touched. He offered me his seat. I didn't take it.

Margaret Atwood spoke of her youth and the nothingness of her summer days. She showed a slideshow of her childhood journal. She was a writer who liked nature and art.

Joyce Carol Oates was pale with dark hair. She made delicate and hypnotic gestures with her hands. Her humor surprised me since I expected her words to be as sharp and terrifying as her fiction. When she spoke of Robert Frost I held my breath. Then I laughed again.

I am the namesake of Nikki Giovanni. My father had once, only once, seen Robert Frost. There are other authors I have seen and will see. I usually wear my best dress. I try to make each occasion a very big deal.

My dad is gone. I will continue to count his birthdays so he will age with me.

I never knew Robert Frost, but I often have miles to go before I sleep.

If I really looked at the details, I would see that neither of them were perfect. Maybe that's why I write. Nothing makes such a beautiful story as broken things and hope. I can still hear their voices. I wish it was always a happy thing, but it's not. Today, it is a terrible absence and connection. I'll try to remember all the details I can. I'll try to keep my glass half-full.

WHAT SALLY SAW

It's been a long time since I've had anyone sleep in my house who wasn't a blood relative or a kid under the age of 10. So when Sally said she was coming, I began to panic.

She won't tell you what she saw. She is too nice. Too Southern. Too proper. But I know what she saw. I hope she will still be my friend.

There are 50 pairs of shoes at the front door. Only 12 of the pairs represent shoes that actually fit on the feet in the house. Of the 12 pairs of shoes, four pairs are cleats. I have hidden an air freshener nearby.

I now have air fresheners all over the house. Behind toilets, under side tables, next to the litter box. We have lived 10 good years in sweet baby scents. Babies smell delicious. Breast milk and baby's breath and even baby tears are maple scented.

Our living room is used for homework. Our dining room is used for piano. We hardly use anything the right way. I take Sally to the kitchen. The oven window is our mirror for dance parties. Inside the pantry, a shoe organizer hangs filled with granola bars and tea bags and ketchup packets. It does not look the way Real Simple promised it would look.

I show her where we keep the plates and glasses. I usually eat cereal out of the sugar bowl. We have no need of a sugar bowl. It is the perfect size for my Raisin Bran.

I can only vouch for half of the food in the fridge. Sally is okay with this. She says the rule in her house is, "Check the date." We are both mothers. We can attest to the fact that we have not yet mastered the art of aligning date purchased and date consumed.

We drink bottled water when we have it. When Sally visits we don't. These are the days we drink tap water. I don't trust the news enough to believe what is said of anything. Bottled water is wasteful and lacks minerals. Tap water is full of chemicals and your old prescription medicine. I divide my loyalties on water and all things. I am carb-free, gluten free, and vegetarian except for the days I eat cake and meat.

I offer her ice from a bag in the fridge. I like science fiction, but our lives are devoid of any automated things. I don't mind the clutter of shoes, but I wish I had a nice fridge that makes ice and water and soda water. I've been looking at one that costs the same as a small car, but I want it anyway.

When Sally sees my kitchen, she doesn't see my dream fridge. She sees a fridge with magnetic poetry and kid artwork and the invitation to a birthday party we forgot to attend.

Upstairs, I lament other things. A sign on the laundry room that warns of the cat, Greg Maddux, who emerges long enough to show Sally some feline indifference. Sally knows about cows and tractors, and maybe a little about barn cats. City cats are different beasts. I shoo Sally away before the hissing starts.

They say I will remember these years with fondness. I will. But right now every inch of my house smells like urine. Between the cat and the children, I've had enough of pee. I would give up my dream fridge for a day free of pee. I tell Sally this. Then I lead her to her room.

It is the best room on the house. Two twin beds. The room that smells least like pee. This room contains all the Barbies and all the LEGOs that haven't escaped to other rooms. Sally is agile enough to watch her step. And her room comes equipped with an aquarium nightlight.

I give Sally clean sheets and towels. I wash a load of laundry every day of my life. On the days I don't wash a load of laundry, I wash three loads. The good news is that Sally can have any kind of soap or shampoo or conditioner. I travel enough to have fancy brands and no-name brands from all kinds of hotels. I cannot resist the lure of hotel body wash. I must have been planning on Sally visiting one day.

The toilet next to her room likes to half-flush in the middle of the night. It is nothing mystical or mysterious. It's a glitch in the system. These are things that are impossible for me to see on any other day. Our lives are like an impressionistic painting. I should have told Sally, my sweet Sally, to take a step back and soften her gaze. This is the only way our world seems perfect. Don't look too closely.

NAKED PICTURES OF ME

When I saw a headline about another celebrity exposed for naked photos, I looked at my feet. I wear wool socks nearly year round. I have poor circulation, and this is why I don't have any naked pictures of myself floating around the internet. I literally and figuratively have cold feet.

I envy the naked selfie people. I grew up swimming in a tee-shirt over my swimsuit. Even my mother thought this was ridiculous. She was from the mini-skirt generation, and I was the baggy-saggy pants generation. We wore our jeans two sizes too big and our flannel shirts with a hoodie, even in the summer. Back then, I never wanted my photo taken with my clothes on. It never occurred to me to take naked pictures. Think about the damage my ex-boyfriend could do with that Polaroid. Tape it inside his locker?

These days naked pictures travel fast. Almost as fast as funny cat videos. I wish I could embrace my inner naked. I should take some naked pictures of myself. We should all take naked pictures of ourselves, so naked celebrity photos stop being newsworthy. Then no one can hold power over someone else just for being in her own skin.

I have a feminist rant about these pictures being used against women.

I have a puritanical rant about why the heck women are

taking so many naked pictures of themselves.

I have an equality rant about the lack of naked male pictures. Remember, the one with Brad Pitt? I do. I'll save those rants for another day.

I'm not judging the naked pictures. Do whatever works for you, but aren't there professional naked people? People who get paid to be naked? I love these people. I thank these people. They exist so I never have to get naked.

There is beautiful art with naked people. Thank you Botticelli and Michelangelo. I'm not sure why it has to be a secret dirty thing.

I had to take some fatty pictures of myself for a fitness challenge. Yes, I said fatty, even though it's really excess skin. No one believes me. I've had four kids. After baby number three, the skin decided, "Why go back?" I want to change the definition of skinny to mean too much skin, but no. Semantics.

I was not happy taking the fatty pictures. At the end of the challenge, my after picture will be a picture of me with my gut sucked in and better posture. If I decide to be an overachiever, I'll add fake eyelashes which are better than weight-loss anyway. If you are staring at my eyeballs, you will not notice my belly skin.

Now I have my not-quite-naked, not-quite-selfie. In the olden days, other people took pictures for you. And I realize the thrill isn't the nudity at all, but the danger of being exposed. There is a thrill in being sexy.

Get down on all fours? That's how you find the missing LEGOs. Twerk? That's how you reduce labor pain. Nudity? It gets you pregnant. Then pregnant gets you naked in front of a long line of doctors and midwives and breastfeeding coaches. Breastfeeding means naked breasts at the sushi restaurant in the square, but at least your baby isn't crying.

I have mixed feelings about being naked. My friends want me to go to that naked spa, which is really a lovely Korean bath house. Guess what? I can't go. I'm not ready yet. I'm not even scared of the naked photos of me. I'm scared because I have cold feet. They won't let you wear wool socks. I know. I called. I asked.

FIRST FRIEND

Second grade was a year of change for me. It was my first year in Georgia. In Connecticut, our friends were Italian and Polish and Jewish. It was not strange to be from Jamaica. Everyone was from somewhere until we moved South. In Georgia, it was only white and black. You might have been from Waycross or Norcross, but certainly not another country.

The black and white truth is that my second grade teacher hated me. She would not call on me when I raised my hand. She despised the sound of my voice. I could see her face shutdown and her body become impatient when I spoke, so I opted not to talk or answer. Even now I know instantly when someone doesn't like me. I learned early. Those things you don't forget.

You don't forget the good things either. We had a beautiful yard surrounding our Georgia house. A perfect expanse of fescue, the softest grass, the most welcoming. And even though I kept my shoes on, I can't tell you the number of times I pressed my face to that Georgia lawn wondering if this place would be home.

I made my first friend in second grade. I don't remember when we met. But I do remember that when she arrived our teacher adored her. When she raised her hand, the teacher called on her. She got to answer. Her work was perfect. Her handwriting sure. She wasn't just smart and pretty, though she was those things, but she was also good. Deep down good and kind. When you are seven years old not much matters other than kindness and mutual laughter. We had that.

We wore the halves of a broken heart necklace in the early years. When the sides met, the heart said "best friends." It didn't need to say forever. Somewhere along the jagged line was eternity.

I wish I could explain to my kids the importance of these first friends in their lives. All of my friends since have been modeled after my first best friend.

We last saw each other as teenagers. Our guess is that we spent the first half of our lives together and the second without. Then I saw her for the first time since high school. I wanted to cry. I did cry. Both of our eyes filled with tears outside of the airport.

I am still silly and snarky, and she is still kindness and goodness. We talked without preamble. She knows everything there is to know about the person I was, the person that history can't change.

We were supposed to marry boys named Jason and Jeremy. I would have three sons, and she would have a boy and a girl. Of course we would live in mansions and drive convertibles and be perfect. Her only fault as a child was not liking tomatoes, and I thought of this as she served me dinner accompanied by a Caprese salad. Only little things had changed.

Our fortunes had not materialized the way we expected. I held her babies who smiled at me to prove that our current lives might be better than what we had hoped for.

When I think back, I wonder how or why we became friends. The kid in me remembers the laughter. The adult in me thinks logically. We were the only brown girls in that class. Maybe we had to be friends. We didn't have a choice. Her family came from India. Our food looked and smelled similar. We both had two brilliant older sisters. She lent me her copy of *The Lion, the Witch, and the Wardrobe* by C.S. Lewis. We loved adventure. We wanted to escape.

Friendship is not a simple connection of being alike. It is often a game of chance all through life. I feel lucky she chose me. How do you ever make friends as an adult? How do you get chosen by another for a lunch date or a shared secret or pain? Who will still be your friend when parts of you change?

I have college friends and neighborhood friends and the occasional friends from work. It is so difficult to make connections in the jaded rush of adulthood. Difficult, but not impossible. I know instantly when someone might be a new friend. I learned that early. Age seven. Those things you always remember.

I look for similarities and differences and jagged lines that, brought together, make connections.

TRAVELS WITH BONO

I stood in the airport baggage claim and could not recall what city I'd arrived from. The monitor showed a list of places. Baltimore, Buffalo, Greensboro, Costa Rica, London, Madrid, Miami, Minneapolis, Orlando. Raleigh, Salt Lake City, D.C. I could have been anywhere. After a moment, I found my boarding pass. It said Charlotte.

I think I am a good traveler. Buena. Bon. Gute.

I prefer a backpack to a suitcase. I travel light. I don't want to drag baggage behind me.

I look forward to taxi rides. I'm not scared of speed or sudden stops or the rage dance of driving in another city. I like new voices. I like the quick questions and quiet revelations the driver makes. Life in another country. Life here. Family.

Twice this year, I've received a hug from the cab driver when I reached my destination. We are all wanderers.

On the airplane, I like the window seat when I plan to write and the aisle seat when the flight lasts more than two and a half hours. I don't trust my bladder after two and a half hours. I don't trust my ability to sit still.

If the person in the middle seat is bigger than me, I will offer to switch seats. I have a soft spot in my heart for tall men scrunched in small space. It's like they feed us the Eat

Me cake from Alice's Wonderland right before we get on the airplane. Everyone is two sizes too big just before take-off.

I don't mind crying babies. I am used to the sound. I don't like it, but I accept it. I wonder why passengers get mad at the sound of sadness. My guess is that it's jealously. Tired babies get to cry it out. Tired adults wish they could do the same.

When the sky is perfectly blue, there is the most turbulence. You need a few clouds to smooth out rough air. If that isn't an old adage, it should be a new one.

I've spent half a day delayed at the airport watching flashes of lightning strike the runway. Not one person in 12 hours complained about the delay.

I see cities from above. Many times we touch down where land and water meet. I imagine there are more piloting skills needed for this even though I know that's not true. I only need wheels down, safe landing, and I'm alive.

I have driven on dark roads after arriving in a strange city. I don't like being lost. I recently plugged in my phone for better directions and suddenly Bono's voice filled the car. I'd forgotten about the free music U2 sent to my phone like magic. I'm not mad at Bono. My mother taught me to say thank you for any gift. Even free ones. Especially free ones.

I've lived my entire life U2 and Bono free. U2 was the LOL, WTF, and TTYL of yesteryear. Me, too? Yes, U2. I've never been a fan, but I am one now. Bono was singing to me. His voice came at just the right time in my traveling exhaustion and despair.

Bono makes a good travel companion. Bonovox. Good. Bueno. I found the hotel 30 minutes later thanks to him. Don't be mad at Bono. I bet he is just like me. Looking for intersections.

As soon as I stepped out of the car, Bono disappeared. I walked into the hotel singing a verse from the Eagles. Admittedly, "Hotel California" is not the best song for a weary traveler, but Bono got me started and you have to do things to entertain yourself when you are far from home.

You may see scenes from airports and hotels and lonely

dinners in future stories. Just assume it's all based on the truth. I never know what might happen when I pack my bags.

ALL KINDS OF PANIC

The more people panic, the less I panic. I've been watching amateurs become experts on infectious diseases. Ebola. Flesh-eating bacteria. Airborne sicknesses. Out of a 100 friends, 90 know for certain how to cure certain diseases and prevent future outbreaks. Strangely enough, the other 10 are my friends who actually work at the CDC.

I am constantly anxiety-ridden and worried about some silly thing. I'm afraid of mascara and high heels over two inches. I'm scared that a bird will fly into my house when I open the front door. You can't tell me this is irrational because it has happened to me before. I understand panic.

When I see other people getting hysterical about strange things, I would never tell them to "just calm down." Panicking is normal. Irrational, but normal. Sometimes the best way to combat hysteria is with more hysteria. These are the main types of panic I see each day.

1. Road rage. You panic because someone wants to merge in front of your car. You should definitely honk your horn and give them the middle finger. You obviously own the road directly in front of your car. You should panic and rage about cars changing lanes and driving too slow or too fast. When you get to the next red light and the offending car is parked right next to you and contains your boss, your wild and profane gestures will seem justified.

2. Babies on an airplane. I'm on airplanes a lot, and you should see the panicked expressions of my fellow passengers when a family boards with a baby. Babies should stay at home. If they leave home, babies should never cry. Your panicked energy and anger directed at that small, and yet rapidly growing, humanoid is not weird at all.

3. Being healthy. No matter how nice your friends are, as soon as you start dieting or exercising, one of your friends is going to start panicking. These are the friends who know all about the dangers of over exercising and make sure to always offer you a piece of cake. Especially at work where all cakes hide. Change is frightening to some people. It is best to distract them with other irrational fears like germs.

4. Germs. Diseases. Bacteria. Viruses. I am not an expert, but I do have 90 expert friends. The only thing I have gleaned from these experts is that we are all going to die. And they are correct.

5. Being right. Some people have to be right. All. The. Time. I'm sure those right people will be the first to comment on this article with why I am wrong. I am constantly wrong in very public and tangible ways, but most people are right all the time. You are right about giving the middle finger to that car while driving. You are right about knowing the best ways to correct society's ills and controversies. The good news is that everyone is always right. Except me. I'm always wrong. I'm wrong, and I'm not panicking about it.

6. Natural Disasters. Let's start planning for snowmageddon now. You know it is coming. We should really worry about it now, while it is still 70 degrees outside. I've got recipes for French toast and bread pudding for days. That's how long we'll be trapped. And panicking. In February. Two whole days.

7. Alien invasions including zombies. I'm more worried that this won't happen.

8. Definitions of success. Are we successful because we work and make money? Are we successful because we have prioritized personal satisfaction over material wealth? Once I make enough money I will definitely prioritize personal satisfaction over material wealth.

9. Spending money on the right/wrong things. I recently had someone complain to me bout the cost of her mammogram. We should celebrate and take care of our ta-tas, and she thought $200 for a mammogram was ridiculous. Her panic was palpable. In the meantime, she is holding an $800 phone. That's when I really started panicking. Do you know how many mammograms you could get for the cost of that phone? Yes, you do. See the simple math above.

10. Fake news. The wonderful thing about today is that we are panicking about news that is not true. Steven Spielberg shoots dinosaur. Pickup truck saves airplane from crash landing. The zombie apocalypse is coming. We should be aware of the types of fake news that cause us to panic. Manipulated photos. Satire that passes as real news. First you believe it, and then you get mad. Don't be mad. Don't panic. Being humorless is serious business.

I don't panic about Ebola or Ecoli or someone driving slowly in the fast lane. I worry about how ticklish my feet are when I get a pedicure. I panic at the thought of cats who can unlock doors. My cat has done this. It worries me. I panic at 4:17 p.m. every day for no good reason. When I see piece of cake I panic. Then I calm down. For now, I am happy and relaxed. I don't have a worry in the world because you are panicking for me. When you all stop panicking, then I'll really worry.

CHANGING MY FACE

I have two noticeable scars on my face. Both occurred when I was little, about five. One looks like a birthmark. The other is clearly a small slash where I got half a dozen stitches. Because I've had the scars most of my life, I don't see them when I look at my face.

From an equally young age, well-intentioned people advised me that I could fix my scars when I got older. "When you get to be 18, you can have a little surgery to fix that." I've been thinking about plastic surgery since I was five years old.

And yet when people have asked me about my scars over the years, I'm always confused. "What scars?" I ask. Some people are born to focus on their imperfections. They can't help it. Others can't see their own scars and blemishes. I'm the latter. By the time I turned 18 years old, I knew I would not have plastic surgery on my scars.

I had my first professional photos taken a few years ago. The photographer had photoshopped away my two scars. I asked her to put them back. It didn't look like my face without the scars. I never see my scars, but without them I don't look like myself. I don't need perfection. Or maybe I do.

What is perfection? People are mad at Renee Zellweger for altering her face. I don't feel bad for celebrities. Naked pictures leaked onto the internet. Accusations of plastic surgery. Celebrities live a life of scrutiny, but so do we regular people. Regular women have to deal with face-shaming daily. At least celebrities get paid for it.

How is makeup less offensive than plastic surgery? I detest mascara and lipstick. I wear mascara grudgingly because I have gray eyelashes. I recently liberated my mouth from lipstick. I hate lipstick because it tastes gross. Why must I wear makeup on my mouth? That's my pie hole. I eat food there. Makeup, please stay away from my mouth. I wear simple lip balm. That's it. I save lip gloss for my MILFy days. Not lipstick. Ever again.

On one of those days that required makeup, my boss told me I looked beautiful and called out to the rest of the office, "Come see Nicki's face!" She said this out loud. My co-workers gathered round to see my supermodel face. That was when I realized I normally look like Nanny McPhee. I even have the moles. On any normal day you can see my scars, bumps, and wrinkles.

By the time I had kids, I began to dream about plastic surgery again, specifically a tummy tuck. I'm so skinny, you know all that extra belly skin. I want it gone. I'm not ashamed to say I want a little nip and tuck.

I know people who have had tummy tucks and lifts and reductions. You can't tell me these are bad things. They have improved the lives of people I know. I've never walked around with DD cups so I can't imagine that life. When my friend decided to show me her post reduction surgery results, I was surprised. She was physically and mentally lighter. I just wished she had given me a little warning. I love breasts as much as the next woman, but I'm a prude. I need at least a three minute warning before you flash me the twins.

These days, my face offers me different woes. Adult acne. Each zit means a new scar or a blemish as the cosmetic people like to say. No one told my life would be filled with scars and concealer and stitches and dreams of plastic surgery.

I wrote an entire novel about a woman with scars on her face, and I can't tell you how many readers asked me why she didn't just get plastic surgery. Are we for plastic surgery or against it? Is plastic surgery bad because we refuse to age gracefully and embrace our wrinkles and saggy bits? Everyone seems to like me better when I hide the wrinkles, suck in the jiggly parts, and push up the saggy parts. "Come see!" Are you mad at the actress for having plastic surgery? Or are you jealous because she did it?

I've never worried about the shape of my eyes or nose. I've never worried about my scars old and new. I'm not one to judge those who do the surgery and those who don't. Who knows what will happen to me when I'm fabulously rich. And bored. Some of us are going to walk around with scars for the rest of our lives. Some of us are going to use our bodies like canvases. We are going to alter ourselves. Good thing I will never be rich or bored. My face is going to change no matter what I do.

A LIFE IN YEARS

I started my year with reflections and optimism. For me, optimism is not a natural thing. I'm a gloom and doom person. I have to try to be positive. I work at being happy like it's my day job. I don't think about the future much. The future is just going to happen to me. I can try to live without regret, but regrets will happen, so I savor the past. I pick out the good from what has happened, and hope for the good in what is yet to come.

I am now the big 4-0. If you ask me, I will tell you how old I am and how much I weigh. I made a promise to myself five years ago that I would never hide my age or weight ever again. I am reflecting on forty good years. Good doesn't mean perfect. Good means I've had a little bit of heartache and sadness and surprises and joy. Not too much of anything is a good life for me. My biography will be blissfully short. My life will be measured in years.

Forty years ago, I was born on a tiny island in the middle of the pale blue sea. Thirty-eight years ago, we flew to a country that I love as much as the land of my birth. I may not be able to be President here, but my kids might. Twenty-two years ago, I ran away to California because I wanted to see oceans and mountains, big valleys and yellow prairies. I found an ever-present chill in the air. That sounds like a bad thing, but it's not. It was refreshing and startling at times. Not all places are a warm blanket like my Georgia home.

Twenty years ago, he asked me if I would be his girlfriend. I told him "No" even though I liked him. Fourteen years ago, he asked if we should get married. I asked him if he meant to each other. He did. Eleven years ago, we thought it would be funny to have a cat named after Greg Maddux.

Ten years ago, we nicknamed my pregnant stomach Lucky. Eight years ago our luck ran out, and there was a baby who didn't make it. Seven years ago, our daughter became 7 of 9 grandkids. If you can raise your kids on *Star Trek* jokes and baseball references they might turn out okay. We won't know if this is true for another twenty years.

Four years ago, we had that nice trip to Puerto Rico and came home expecting baby number four. The surprise baby. No one told me I would cry equally for the ones I would have and the one I lost. Three years ago, she was born on a day it snowed. I thought I was going to die. Two years ago, someone thought they might like to buy my novel. A year and a half ago, I did not have to have that biopsy.

Last year, I turned thirty-nine. On my birthday, I ate a pound of crab legs with my mom and dad and husband. I stood in the morning light of Piedmont Park and watched my kids run across a completely empty meadow. Two weeks later, my father died. I used to be ashamed to cry, but now I'm not.

We survived last Thanksgiving Day with dirt from the cemetery still on our shoes. I spent every day of this year learning to navigate overwhelming grief and disappointment. I've learned to look for happiness. I've learned to let happiness find me.

Today, though I like him a lot, I would never call my husband my best friend. He knows this. But I am still his girlfriend. I write to make sense of the world. When it rains my kids say, "Mommy, isn't this your favorite kind of day?" I like sunshine, and I like shadows. I do laundry like I'm fighting the plague. I love birthdays. I don't wish for anything, because I never get what I wish for. I put myself in uncomfortable situations on purpose. I find feeling comfortable unsettling. I have watched grief and happiness become good friends in my life. I often see them holding hands.

What is a life? We count the days and years between our birth and death. We count candles. We blow out the flames. But I don't like to. I'd rather keep track of the years. I'd rather keep the candles burning.

THE THING ABOUT BUBBAS

I took a drive to Augusta, Georgia, and it's no surprise that I met a Bubba there. I meet Bubbas everywhere. They find me.

I grew up in Stone Mountain. There was a Bubba in my high school. He played some kind of sport. I was not friends with that Bubba, but I made assumptions about him based on his name. Boys named Bubba don't like *Star Trek* or poetry or eating spicy food. I assumed that after high school there would be no more Bubbas in my life. I was wrong.

Years ago, I was on a flight from Atlanta to San Francisco and happened to sit among a trio of men. They wore work boots and still had the dust from a day's work stuck to their sunburnt faces. I didn't need to see beneath their collars to know their necks were red. As I buckled in, I began to worry. The man next to me was nervous about flying. All three of them seemed to be inexperienced travelers. I had a book I wanted to read and a crossword puzzle to tackle and five hours trapped in the air with these guys.

The first thing they did was introduce themselves. They were from Shreveport, Louisiana.

"I'm Bubba, that's Bubba over there, and this is *Buddha*," one said to me. Two Bubbas I could understand, but the third had reached full spiritual enlightenment? I'd watched enough of the TV show *Newhart* to wonder if this was a joke. Had they just Larry, Darryl, and Darryled me? They assured me it was the truth. They were co-workers going to work on the Alaska pipeline.

One of the Bubbas had taken a short flight within Louisiana one time. It was Buddha's first time on an airplane.

A business man in the row ahead of us turned his body in our direction, and I could tell he was paying attention to our introductions in case something uncomfortable happened. I didn't belong with these Bubbas, but nothing uncomfortable happened. I seemed worldly to them. "You must be smart," the other Bubba said has he looked at my book. It was a historical romance novel.

I closed the book and invited them to talk to me. They wanted to talk. I thought it was to calm Buddha's anxiety. Maybe it was. But they were three guys who liked to talk and liked to meet new people and didn't worry about details like being different from me.

During that five hour flight, I learned about fishing and what brings three men to leave home for six months. They claimed Shreveport was a very small city. Too small for these Bubbas, but they had a lot of affection for their families and friends back home. After talking for only an hour, they had a lot of affection for me, too.

"Is your boyfriend nice to you?" they asked. They watched my face closely when I responded. Each man bowed up like warriors who might have to go kick some ass when the plane landed.

"He is nice," I told them. Bubba, Bubba, and Buddha relaxed visibly, and we continued to talk for five hours. My book sat unread. I never started the crossword puzzle. I figured Buddha would not be nervous on his next flight.

I put on some makeup as the plane started to descend. "You do not need makeup," Buddha said. One of the Bubbas agreed. "You're pretty without it." Every once in a while I hear Buddha's voice when I look at mascara.

There have been lots of Bubbas in my life since then.

There have been Skips and Chips and Juniors and Billy Bobs, but they don't hold a candle to the Bubbas.

I was at a book event, and as I set up a burly, bearded, tattooed man approached. "Are you Nicki Salcedo?" he asked me, and then handed me an envelope. There are a lot of assumptions you can make about a woman named Nicki. That Prince song has not helped me. Then again maybe it has. Nicki is either naughty or a cheerleader or both. I admit that the edgy parts of my wardrobe come from The GAP, and I smell like IKEA.

I give off enough warning signs that Bubbas should stay away from me. They should assume that I don't love football or conversations on a plane. But Bubbas know better than that.

When I opened the envelope, I found a birthday card for me signed by Bubba and his girlfriend. She is an avid reader. They drove from Tuscaloosa, Alabama to Augusta, Georgia to attend a book event. He called me "ma'am" in that polite sweet way that Northern women can't appreciate. He carried a box for me. He told me the story of how he met his girlfriend. I signed a book for them.

My new friend Bubba is a tattoo artist. He probably noticed that I have none. The closest thing I have to a tattoo are some scars on my face. One is shaped like two moons. He probably noticed that I am different from him, but he did not judge me for my silly name or the things I am and am not.

Bubba is a derivation of the word "Brother" and having only sisters, a brother is a nice thing to have every now and then. That's the thing about Bubbas. Every now and then a Bubba just might brighten your day.

WHAT I BURIED

Advice comes whether or not you want it. When I get guidance, I ignore it. I'm not good at following directions. When I'm given instructions, I do the opposite. I start my New Year's resolutions in July or September. Never in January. When November comes, I refuse to be thankful. Now more than ever.

My father's funeral was last year on the day before Thanksgiving. A terrible coldness passed through the city. The wind held doors open that needed to be shut and closed doors when someone tried to come in. The white sky warned of snow and none fell.

I was not thankful standing over my father's coffin. He was good enough to be liked and remembered. He was human enough that my grief was clouded by anger. He and my mother taught us to be grateful because nothing is promised. Except death.

I should have been thankful for our friends who attended the funeral, but I wasn't. It is the wrong day to see loved ones.

"I'm so sorry to see you under these circumstances," everyone said.

I thought, "You should be sorry." Every time. Then again, I did feel comforted by people who knew me all my life, before I was a woman or wife or mother.

One particular person changed my perspective that day. This woman and I grew up together. Even though we weren't close, her parents were like mine. Mine were like hers. When her mother died fourteen years ago, I flew back to Atlanta from San Francisco because I had to say goodbye. This childhood friend gave advice, and for the first time I listened.

"It will never get better," she whispered as she gave me a hug. I found her honesty comforting.

Other people said, "It takes time" and "You have a lot to be thankful for." True and true. I am thankful for the man who did small things. He sang in a deep resonating voice. He made pancakes every weekend. He planted a rose bush that flowered three months after he died. I stood at my mom's front door hating the beautiful flower.

I don't discount optimistic advice, but when my dad died I wanted another kind of truth. I wanted someone to say that a year later my grief would still be an open sore. I needed to hear that I should dig a grave for the parts of me that died with my dad.

I've buried many things this year. Hesitation. Silence. Fear of big things, though I've kept the ability to worry over small things. I buried looking at my life like there's a finish line. I buried feeling inadequate. I buried saying "yes" and put a hatchet in it.

I buried my father's mistakes. I make enough of my own. I should bury those, too. But not yet. I threw in the whole world for its infinite attempts to discourage and distort. I buried happiness and sadness being two separate things. I buried thank you.

I will not be thankful for the obvious this November. I love my family and my job and my friends, but I am thankful for unexpected and unusual things. My father and my mother taught us to be thankful because everything is precious. Even the blades of grass. Even a lonely flower.

I think of all the digging my father did for those roses. Forgive me for not being very thankful for this November.

Forgive me for wishing he could see the one single flower that dared to blossom. Forgive me for being thankful for the petals, but grieving too much to touch them.

Last year, I did not want Thanksgiving. I did not want Christmas. I wanted to dig an extra grave and fill it with all the things wrong in my life. I am still tender and raw. I am still changing. I am, in my own way, thankful. When I look at the ground, I don't see graves. I don't see death. I am waiting for something to bloom.

DON'T BLAME BARBIE, BLAME CPT. KIRK

Barbie is the queen of controversy. For the love of all things sacred, she is not human. She's a toy. I want people to leave Barbie alone.

Sure, the book "Barbie: I Can Be a Computer Engineer" was a tragic mistake of Shakespearean proportions. It was. This misogynistic story suggests that Barbie cannot be a computer engineer. This is not Barbie's fault. I bet the person who wrote the book never owned a Barbie. Blame that person. Blame Ken. Tell him to get a job.

Blame Captain Kirk. Nothing about his life is realistic.

I loved my Barbies. They were hand-me-downs from my sisters. My first brand-new Barbie was Christie. She was black and a supermodel, and she came with a camera. If you pushed a button on her back, she'd strike a pose. I loved her. I loved all my Barbies, blonde and blue-eyed and with that incredible thigh-gap. It didn't matter to me.

Barbie was make believe. In my real life, I spent my time digging in my backyard. I liked bugs. I mowed the lawn. I knew how to edge and reseed the grass. I knew how to trim the shrubbery. I liked Alfred Hitchcock movies and *The Twilight Zone* and *Star Trek* and cowboy books by Louis L'Amour. There were a lot of male influences on me from a young age. Bionic men, motorcycle cops, or good old boys

driving cars with doors that didn't work. Barbie was a
godsend.

Barbie was better than all those men. She was a doctor,
veterinarian, rock star, and astronaut. She got $hit done, and
she got it done while wearing stilettos. Ken never did
anything. My Barbie found his presence distasteful. My
Barbie didn't need Ken. She didn't need Captain Kirk either.

Captain Kirk can't be a computer engineer even though
he's from the future. He'd ask Sulu for directions and make
Spock code. But nobody ever complained about Kirk being
unrealistic or incompetent. He isn't a real person. And who
wants reality? I like my Kirk the way I like my Barbie.
Imaginary.

Kirk needs to be a better role model. He tries to mate with
every alien woman he meets. He fails to value intelligence in
women. Does he know what a dilithium crystal is? Kirk gets
the Enterprise out of danger by using everyone else's skills on
the ship. He is just a pretty boy figurehead leading us on
intergalactic adventures that ultimately culminate in success.
If I wanted reality this would be preposterous. Do we want
our heroes to be as spirit crushing? Do they need to be
realistic?

No one gets mad at Kirk. No one hates James Bond. No
one complains that he's got a drinking problem. He's an
international spy wearing a tuxedo? I would pretty much
notice him if he walked into my casino. He is handsome and
fit with his exotic accent. Now my son feels inadequate. He
wants his hot chocolate shaken, not stirred. He will never
become a waif, British, gadget-carrying hero. My son cries
himself to sleep at night thanks to Bond. James Bond.

I do have a few complaints about Barbie. She contributed
to my naiveté lasting longer than it did for other girls. When I
learned about sex my first thought was, "That's not how my
Barbie had sex!" *What goes where?* Ken and Barbie had the
same anatomy except the boobs. Let's be clear, what Barbie
had were not breasts. There were no nipples. I figured my
breasts would grow into something Barbie-like as I matured.

But no, the nipples did not fall off. They stayed. When I had babies, these breast-nipples things worked in ways Barbie had not prepared me for. Not only is there a spout, but there is a showerhead-like spray. Of milk. Barbie should have told me.

My kids have hand-me-down Barbies from their cousins. These kids will become engineers or rock stars if they want to. I want them to be smart enough to become who they should be. I want them to understand the difference between real and imaginary influences. I'd rather not blame their failures on a plastic doll from 1950 or an oversexed space captain from the year 2200.

The people who hate Barbie probably never had one. Barbie is not perfect. She can't wear flat shoes. It's difficult getting her rigid body in and out of her wonderful outfits. Her hands are stuck in the Vulcan greeting. This explains my crush on Spock and why I blame everything wrong in the world on Kirk.

Don't blame Barbie for my failures. Barbie wants me to be the best I can be. She wants wider sleeves and opposable thumbs. She wants me to live long and prosper.

HIDE THE BATTERIES

The best reason to have kids is to play with toys, but toys are also one of the reasons not to have kids. Don't get me wrong, there are lots of good reasons to not have kids. Poop. Pee. The edge of your shirt being used for boogers. The porta-potty on the soccer field. Lack of sleep.

Toys are a perk and a trap. You bring them into the house under the guise of creating happiness and you end up with is chaos and despair. Consider these issues as you shop for toys this holiday season. I can't tell you to DO or DON'T buy anything. Buy whatever you like, but be aware of the dangers of each toy.

Gender biased toys. Once you conform to the dominant paradigm and buy the Barbie or Ironman action figure, some parents will judge you for perpetuating gender stereotypes. My girls like pink stuff with glitter. My son likes Ironman. Guess what? I am perpetuating gender stereotypes, even though I hate pink and glitter is evil.

If gender biased toys are an issue, I have a solution for you. Rocks are gender neutral. Trees, though phallic, are gender neutral. Or instead of gifts, send your kids to play outside.

Toys with eyes. I love Barbie, because her eyes are too small to be creepy. I never liked baby dolls with eyelids that close when you put them down and open when you pick them up. The original *Twilight Zone* episode "Living Doll" scarred me for life. Talky Tina was not right in the doll brain. Who's afraid of things under the bed when there are plenty of frightening eyeballs staring at you from your toy chest? **Toys with on/off switches.** Noise and movement. We have every kind of buzzing remote control car or zooming superhero. Some toys make noise for no apparent reason, except to rattle the synapses of my brain. I can deal with noise, but eventually dying batteries lead to strange sounds in the middle of the night. Ironman's low battery death is enough to shut down my ovaries. "I am Ironma-ma-ma..." Just die already. Hide the batteries.

Musical instruments are noise with a purpose. We have xylophones, harmonicas, recorders, and drums. My children's music teacher recommended that we get a real guitar with an amp because she hates us.

"We have enough noise sounds in our house. We don't need any kind of sound amplified," I said.

Sure there are headphones, but if headphones were a good solution, that talking Ironman action figure would have come with headphones.

Too many parts. Decks of cards. Uno. Monopoly money. Jigsaw puzzles. The missing piece meets the big "Oh, no you didn't," and I'm looking for the trash can. Games or toys with multiple parts rarely stay together. The pieces revolt. You will find them in distant corners and the sock drawer and the trunk of your car, but never in the same spot after the box is open. Toys with many parts are good for parents who like to play hide-and-seek. I promise you, your kids will never look for these missing pieces.

Very small pieces, otherwise known as vacuum food. I used to panic and dig LEGOs out of the vacuum. Those building sets are expensive, but now my kids know the rules. Anything I pick up goes into the garbage. If a toy gets vacuumed up, it goes to the great beyond. I'm not dumpster diving for a red 2×2 brick ever again. Small pieces are a choking hazard. They are also nose and ear hazards. Medical professionals have extracted all manner of objects from our various head holes. Feed the vacuum and save yourself a trip to the doctor.

Being crafty. I want my kids to learn how to sew and make jewelry, but not inside my house. My sister gave my kids a "create your own marker" set and offered me a half-hearted apology as my daughter opened it. Any gift that comes with "I'm sorry" will make you sorry indeed.

Books. I'm not a toy Grinch. I enjoy The Game of Life even though I despise the little peg people that go in the car. I love Play-Doh. I love magic markers that are used to make artwork on my walls. I've found a great solution for my toy dilemma. I go to the bookstore with my kids. I love to read. I love books. It's time for holiday shopping, and I'm notorious for giving books to my whole family.

Buying books is really the best reasons to have kids. We get to use our imagination. But let's be honest. I like books because they are quiet and clean and cause no destruction.

Don't peek. Here comes the truth. I'm not supposed to like toys. But I do. I like the Barbies even though they are always naked. I like Silly Putty. I like Ironman before his batteries die and when he is still super. There are days when I want to hide the batteries and throw everything in the trash. But I don't. The mess and noise don't matter.

Be the hero. Buy your child or nephew or neighbor whatever YOU want. Aunts and godparents and Nana don't worry about these things. Be a kid again. Don't be a scrooge. Enjoy the pieces and noise. Share in the fun. Enjoy the toys.

DARK ALLEYS

Women are trained from an early age to be gracious, silent, and cautious. When I walk alone, I stay alert. I carry my keys. I avoid isolated areas. I never go out alone when it is very late or very early even in busy areas. I loop around the block. A woman knows what this means. A stranger is on your block or near your home, and you don't want them to know where you live. You loop.

I have to follow the rules. Men don't live this way. They live free. My husband asked me an unsettling question.

"Do you ever feel afraid?" he asked. "As a woman? Are you afraid walking down the street?"

We have known each other for twenty years. We talk a lot. There are no reasons to be coy or circumspect with him, but I didn't know what to say. He had recently read something about the rape culture in America.

"I'm not afraid, but I'm alert." I didn't say much else. I didn't say that I am often afraid, but not in dark alleys. No one prepared me for the places I truly needed to fear.

In college, I was afraid at times. I went to a nice college with smart boys. You are with a group of friends, people come and go, and eventually you are in a room with a different group of friends. Suddenly, you're the only girl in the room. I clearly remember one situation where I thought,

"How do I walk out of here and not seem like I'm afraid?"

It was just as I said. We were not drunk. We had gone to get smoothies. There were several of us, but eventually it was two boys and me. I could hear my mother's voice from three thousand miles away warning me. This was my dark alley.

There were smiles and laughter. A playful tug at my shirt. The tenor of the room changed. I don't remember what I said. I'm sure I made a joke. I'm sure I made every attempt to make them feel comfortable as I left even though I felt unbearably uncomfortable.

College is a time to navigate sexual politics. I might be labeled. Liberated, slut, victim, bitch, or prude. I only wanted be the girl who likes *Star Trek* and Scrabble. I was only prepared to defend myself from strangers.

Even now I find myself in uncomfortable situations.

I am not a hugger. I don't like being touched. I pretty much give off the vibes not to come near me ever, and yet it happens in professional situations. A few years ago, a man put his hand on my knee at a work function. I'm sure he, the married man, thought this was an innocent thing. I didn't. I had to stand up and walk away while using the cheese tray across the room as my excuse. It was on me to deflect unwanted advances, with a smile.

If I say, "Don't touch me," I am being too direct and abrasive. Why am I worried about the feelings of the man who put his hands on me?

If I say, "My husband really loves The Cowboys. . ." I am trying to distract. This says that I am not the right victim, but he can direct his advances to another woman. Why is this acceptable?

If you have not been in these situations, you have wonderful advice for how I should have asserted myself. You don't know. Far too many women do. The moments before rape are often subtle. So our reactions. How do you shout "No!" and rage when it started with a smile and playful tug on your shirt?

Women are coming forward with rape stories, both recent

and decades old. I tend to believe these accounts. I remember the moment when I felt the tenor in the room change. I remember the split second I had to assert myself, with a smile, and get to a safer place. Not all women have that chance.

Women know how to walk through an empty parking garage, but not how to safely exit a frat party or professional situation. Forget dark alleys. How do I warn my daughter about the boy sitting next to her in Chemistry class? Or her work colleague?

When my husband asked me if I'm ever afraid, I should have told him that I am. I should have told him I'm afraid in unexpected places.

Stay alert. Carry your keys. Never use your body to hurt another person. Don't be afraid to walk away. Don't be afraid to shout or rage or make a scene. Don't be afraid to exit quietly, with a joke and a smile.

Boys, whether they are seventeen or seventy, have a split second choice. Power and dominance and fear. Or kindness. They always have a choice, when we don't.

I want men and boys to speak up. We are all accountable, but only men can stop this.

The news has been troubling me. I haven't been raped, but the stories feel familiar to me. I've stayed quiet. Silence and hesitation is the problem. I want to be gracious, silent, and cautious. I want to be those things, but I can't anymore. I buried silence. For me. For my family. For anyone else who needs to be heard.

CAT CHRISTMAS

It is universally known that cats will go to heaven. It's because cats like Christmas. They like Christmas more than dogs. In fact, cats like Christmas better than people. While I am woefully ignorant on pet theology, I feel comfortable knowing that one day Maddux will take the cat door through the pearly gates.

Brandy was our most memorable cat. We got her when I was 11 years old, and she was a teeny tiny kitten during her first Christmas. A kitten Christmas was a tactical error on our part. Brandy took one look at the tree and immediately climbed to the top. She was so little, she didn't knock down the Christmas tree. Brandy just meowed in happiness while swaying on the tree trunk. Many times that season we would have to reach in between the lights and ornaments and extract a kitten from the branches.

Don't bring outside in and expect your pets to act normal.

As the years went by, Brandy got too big to climb the tree, and she turned her feline attention to our Christmas presents. One year, we'd attached stick-on bows to our gifts. Brandy thought the presents looked better plain and systematically removed bows from all the presents and hid them in nearby corners.

My mother switched to using real ribbon the following

year.

Brandy moved on to fighting tinsel. Why did we think that throwing shredded foil all over tree was a good idea? Even if you don't have a cat, this is a colossally bad idea.

I guess part of my Christmas joy has always been watching my cats get ecstatic with Christmas happiness. Flashing lights and a dangling ornament go a long way with a cat. This is why animals are better than people. Animals love the small stuff. Have you ever seen a dog get a new tennis ball? Frisbee? A kid would never get that excited at a disc or sphere.

My cat Maddux no longer likes Christmas the way she did as a kitten.

Our first Christmas with her, I came home and found the top of an ornament and a hook. No glass ball anywhere. At first I could not figure where the glass ornament had gone. This happened for a couple of days before I caught her in the act. The act of eating glass. I was petrified.

I was prepared for the ornaments being knocked off or tinsel batted around. I had never heard of a cat eating glass. Do you know what that equates to in my stress and vet bills?

And she was fine. Not a bit of tragedy there. She ate glass and it didn't bother her one bit.

The next year, I put the glass ornaments higher, but Maddux would always find a way to climb on a table or bookshelf to knock off a glass ball. And eat it. Her iron stomach gave me little comfort. Eating glass was too much for me. I love glass ornaments. I have a collection of beautiful ornaments from Germany that my kids will never see. I have not had a glass ornament on my tree in ten years. Thanks to the cat.

This year when the tree went up, my kids decorated the whole thing on their own. The tree was covered in kid-made ornaments. Paper snowflakes, popsicle stick angels, and felt stockings with glitter-glue names. Maddux sauntered by with disdain. Like Christmas was dead to her.

"You hate Christmas, because you already ate it," I whispered at her, but she ignored me as much as she ignored the tree.

I want Christmas to be fun, and safe, for my cat. She was my first baby. As many stories as I have with my family, I have about my cats. I want the holidays to be joyous. We bring in this huge symbol of outside into the inside. To dogs, it must look like a good place to pee. To cats, it must look like a glimpse of heaven. Cats know the true meaning of Christmas.

Run around like wild, climb a tree, pick fights with inanimate objects, and eat everything in sight. Happy Holidays.

EVE AND AFTER

My oldest sister would choose the firewood. She knew how to find the driest pieces. My other sister sorted through the newspaper and removed the shiny flyers and advertisements. We would stack wood interspersed with paper. We would light the fire and fan the flames. Eventually, we felt heat push back at us. When we turned to each other, we could see firelight reflected in each other's eyes.

I would toss in pine straw and watch it glow without blazing. It would burn red for a moment, then curl into nothing.

Georgia winters were sometimes cold. I remembered it snowed once on Christmas Eve. Other winters were mild, but we always had a fire. We always had our traditions.

Our parents would be in the kitchen. My dad chopped onions and green peppers. My mom seasoned the stuffing and added secret ingredients like mushrooms and celery. I can still hear the sound of her hand patting the turkey with the affection of a woman bathing her child. There was ham and a roast and curry chicken. Broccoli casserole. Rice and peas. No one dish was the centerpiece.

My sisters would tidy the house and bathrooms even if no one was coming. The house had to be perfectly clean. Sometimes I would be assigned to polish the silver. It was a soothing task that helped distract me from the excitement and happiness bursting inside me.

Our house was filled with Christmas music. My husband was surprised when I sang every word to "Tennessee Christmas." All I could think is, "Doesn't everyone know the words to that song?" No Christmas song was off limits. Gospel, Country, George Michael and Wham! If someone made a Christmas album we knew it. We knew the church versions and the pop versions. We would sing as we cooked and cleaned and wrapped. We each had a favorite song. My parents sang beautifully, but my sisters and I sang off key. It didn't matter at Christmas.

As the youngest, I would be sent to bed first. Though we weren't taught to believe in Santa, we weren't taught not to believe. I try to teach my kids the same way. I think you can know the truth and still believe a little bit.

My bed was under the window. I could always see the night sky if I wanted to. I could always listen for sleigh bells.

So we spent our Christmas Eve. Better than Christmas. Together. Waiting.

I never had many gifts to wrap. I had no allowance. As I grew older, my mother would indulge me with the money to buy my sisters fuzzy slippers and robes. My mother would get perfume or bath salts even though we never saw her taking baths. We'd buy my father horrible ties that he'd wear once. After he died, we laughed about the skinny yellow Miami Vice tie he got one year. When I think of my dad it is almost always about Christmas. When people say, "It's the thought that counts" you think they mean gifts, but I think it means making memories.

We never rushed to open our presents. We liked to take our time. When Christmas fell on Sundays, we went to church first before opening any gifts. We were three girls who tried to make Christmas day last as long as possible. We'd eat breakfast first. Maybe peek in our stockings. Our friends would have opened everything before dawn. We moved slowly. We tried to make Christmas morning last forever.

Last year we barely made it through Christmas. It felt like we were clinging on the side of a cliff waiting to fall. I didn't want Christmas or carols or the warmth of firelight. This year, I'm ready.

Christmas Eve is my favorite day of the year. We will wrap gifts that are noisy and require batteries and have small parts. I'll be making a cherry pie. My husband made tamales. I don't have any silver to polish. I don't have to go to bed before midnight, but I might take a peek at the sky before I close my eyes. And listen quietly. Just in case.

1999

When I think back on the best things that happened this year, I end up back in 1998. It was not an exceptional year in any way, except all year we planned to party like it's 1999. On December 31, I was in New York City.

At 3 pm, we walked through Times Square. The crowds were forming. Police officers and barricades lined the streets. It reminded me of end-of-the-world movies when aliens attack. Always in New York City. Atlanta is never attacked by aliens. By 11:59 pm, we were nestled in an Irish pub twenty blocks away. We'd spent the day walking the city in the falling snow.

There was no guide book for how to properly party like it's 1999. I was with my college roommates. We crashed in a two bedroom apartment. Two bedroom meant one room with beds and another room with a sofa, not two separate bedrooms. And eight of us slept in that apartment. What a party.

I'm sure friends will be gathered like that tonight. Wandering the streets the next day and finding good French toast on Lexington made by a real French man in Manhattan. It is possible that 1998 was the best part of my year this year.

Or it could be 1999 was the best part of my year. That was spent in L.A. the night before The Rose Bowl and Y2K.

Instead of an alien invasion, the 2000 apocalypse in Los Angeles was going to be computers malfunctioning and riots in the streets.

The Terminator is my all-time favorite movie. I was not afraid of Y2K. I mentally prepared myself to join the human resistance. We went to Costco around 3 pm. People were buying generators and five gallons of mayonnaise. I had plans to party like two-thousand zero zero party over. It's out of sight.

At 11:59 pm, we were at a restaurant in Pasadena. I did not dance 1999 in or dance 1999 out. That's what happens on New Year's Eve. A lot of build up for nothing.

In 2003, I rang in the New Year with bronchitis and partied with Scrabble and Nyquil. I missed 11:59 pm completely. I fell asleep at ten o'clock at night and woke up at two in the morning. Honestly, 11:59 pm is the most irritating minute of the year. Why are we all watching time like that minute should do a trick or tell a joke?

Each year we hurry out the old to bring in the new, but I think I'd like to cling to this year. Why do we hate the things we've done or haven't done? Why do we want to forget the things that have happened to us? What difference will a minute make?

I keep friends in Australia just for December 31. They'll drag this globe into the next year whether we want to go or not. By the time I open my eyes, Australia has already partied for me. Thank you, Oz! I'm sorry I'm always behind the times.

I remember my New York New Year's Eve just as clearly as the one spent with Nyquil. I'm not sorry to see this year go, even though I should be. It was my first year without my dad. Every day and every holiday marked his absence. If this year ends, I'll only move further away from him.

Then again, this was a good year for so many reasons. My book was published. I had an expected trip to Madrid and an unexpected trip to Costa Rica. If you had told me I was going to travel on 11:59 pm last year, I wouldn't have believed you.

I now expect sadness to come with happiness. I hope for the unexpected. I count on the predictable. Some things happen every year. Time is constant like the waves touching the shore, but even the tide changes. Time is too close. Time is too far away.

My very favorite New Year's tradition is sparkling apple cider and homemade cheese biscuits. I party like it's 1999 every year. I like to wear my pajamas and my wool socks. I like to reminisce about the alien invasion and robot uprising. I like to watch the clock and for a minute feel like Cinderella. There are some of us who don't want the clock to strike midnight.

And there's me, who wants a time machine. May goodness find you in the future and the past.

Happy Old Year. Happy New Year.

CURVE THE LINE

I'm not giving up cake. I won't. I don't do New Year's resolutions ever. If I do them, I do them late in the year and all wrong. This year I feel like I should do things I wouldn't normally do, but do it my way. Instead of making resolutions to diet and organize my closet, I plan to do more of the things I'm already good at. I'm going to be the old me this year. I'm going to do the things I do best.

Curve the line. For a non-coffee drinker I spend a lot of time in coffee shops. It's not for the free Wi-Fi or the insane and overly loud conversations that surround me. I don't go to write the next great American novel, though I should. I go into coffee shops to do one thing. I make sure the line of customers waiting to order beverages curves in the correct direction.

The line at Dancing Goats Coffee Shop in Decatur should curve toward the front doors facing Ponce De Leon Avenue. It should not curve toward the back of the coffee shop. It should not obstruct the pickup zone or the cream and sugar area. I have not had to correct the line in Java Monkey. Maybe it is the stairs or the single entry point. But I have walked into Dancing Goats, corrected the line, and then exited without ordering anything. It's my civic duty. Maybe it should be yours, too. If you join with me on this small resolution in your local coffee shops the world will become a better place.

Eat the apple skin. Eat the apple core. Before I curved lines, I wondered if my existence was to eat only the skin of the apple while passing the fruit along to my offspring. When they were little kids, the apple skin was tough to swallow. I didn't want to peel apples and throw away the skin. I would eat the skin right off the fruit, then hand the apple back to my kid. Now that they are older, they eat the skin and the fruit, but hand the core back to me. I can have my own apple, but sometimes life hands you the tough parts. This year I'm going to perfect eating the core when it is given to me.

Let no one be a stranger. My favorite part about living in the South is the freedom to say hello to anyone, anytime. I resolve to say "hello" to more passing strangers than I have any year before. I like to make up quick stories when someone walks by me. It helps me think that people aren't really strangers.

His dad called him Chipper.

Her dog sleeps next to her left foot.

That's it. Maybe those aren't even stories, but a quick thought. I'll give a passing "hello" and a quick thought. That's what I'll do more of this year.

Remember the difference between trivia and trivial. Trivia is a detail. Trivial is something that's insignificant. If I can spend more time on one and less on the other I'll have a good year. So much of my time is wasted on one disguised as the other.

I'm good at spotting the trivial, but not always avoiding it. I don't need to watch every two minute video that crosses my path. It is important to know certain details, but this year I'll try to stick to the important ones.

Acknowledge the things I'm good at. I am great at precisely five things. Thinking. I think all the time. Mostly about zombies and aliens, time travel, cake, and cats. I'm great at lethargy. I'm great at worrying. I'm excellent at picking the third cutest guy in any ensemble cast and in boy

118

bands. I'm really great at encouraging people to write. I think everyone should write.

For the New Year, I'm leading a series of writing workshops. I've never done anything like this before, but then again here I am making pseudo New Year's resolutions. I'll do some things that I'm good at and some things that are new to me.

We are so busy fixing ourselves in January. By December we are disappointed. We often forget how great we already are.

Don't read the comments. Or the book excerpt. Or movie review. I tend to like things better if I don't know what other people think about them. I recently watched the movie *Snowpiercer*. I had no idea who was in the movie or what it was about. I spent the whole movie wondering, "Is that Captain America and Octavia Spencer?"

Tilda Swinton can do no wrong in my book and the same goes for Ed Harris. Well, now I've ruined the movie for you. You might hate it, but I love seeing expected things. I don't really care if anyone else likes it as long as I did.

See you in December. I plan to look forward to December. It is still part of the New Year. Don't treat it like an over ripe banana. The new me is the permission to be the old me. I will keep the line curved and take a bite out of the core. It's my year to eat cake and be really great at ridiculous things. It can't be hard to resolve to be the ridiculous person you already are.

JE SUIS WRITER

I am a writer. I write fiction. But I'm not a journalist. I don't do satire.

Once a week, I write down my observations of the world. These personal essays are a challenge for me. Fiction is easy. The truth is hard.

I document the intersections where ideas and people meet. I'm simple. I live in a dark corner of Georgia. I write about cats and coffee shops. Even when contemplating the mundane, my words have power. All words do.

Words can kill. Words can get you killed.

I write with two objectives: be gracious and tell the truth. Some writers use their words and ideas to alienate and stir controversy. Some writers have no intention of being kind or careful with their words.

I, too, have caused irritation with my words. I've been called a racist, a hand-wringing anti-feminist, and a stay-at-home-mom. The strange thing about being called a stay-at-home-mom is that the comment was meant as an insult, and I'm not a stay-at-home-mom. You can't trust detractors. They will interpret my words the way they want, no matter my intentions.

I don't let the comments silence me. I don't get angry when I see opinions that differ from my own. The purpose of writing is to start a conversation, not create uniform agreement. I take issue with satire that goes too far. I question satire that is meant to shock and insult. I wonder what thoughtful conversation might come out of it.

I respect the creative process. I believe in the freedom of speech. I don't want anyone to be censored. I don't want anyone to die.

A dozen people died in France and two thousand died in Nigeria. What is freedom? What is art? What is terror? I write to find answers.

Here is the terrible reality. All words are dangerous. If you write satire or stir controversy, if you write humor or memoir, if you tell lies for the sake of gaining readers or tell the truth for the sake of losing them. No matter what you write, you will challenge someone's belief system. You will hurt feelings. You will evoke rage.

I believe everyone should write. Write poetry, a letter to your grandmother, a compliment to the staff at the coffee shop. Write words. Get a pen. Bloody the paper. When you write you become a better reader.

I am careful when I write, but I won't censor myself. I'm not looking for agreement, but intersections. I'd love to see an editorial from someone on why the line in the coffee shop should curve the other way. I like to see different points of view.

I am not French. I am not Nigerian. I mourn loss of life whenever I read the news. I avoid the news because it is selective. I don't believe it all to be true. It feeds my sadness and disappointment. Writing gives me joy and hope.

I am a writer. Je suis writer. I write about things close to me. That grave east of Stone Mountain. The lush green grass in my backyard from thirty years ago. I think about things far away. An office building containing a massacre. Bloody pens on the floor. I think about stories that are never told. Missing women and children. Bodies destroyed by fire.

I should be afraid to write. I'm not. Je suis writer. I realize I'm not afraid of dark alleys. I'm not afraid of anything.

Especially words.

THE FALCONS AND ME

There are two things I don't cry over: football and politics. I support. I vote. But I know my team's limitations. And I still believe in winning.

Every year when football season ends, I am tempted to write a letter to my team to apologize for the things I've done that contributed to our losses. Why should winning be dependent on the athleticism of the players and the strategy of the coaches? It has a lot to do with me wearing my lucky shirt and whether or not I watched the game.

I am not superstitious about anything except football. I have a black cat. She might be named for a baseball player, but she is quite a lucky cat. I open umbrellas inside. I always walk under ladders. I can't resist the urge to tempt fate. But don't mess around with football.

I have regrets for last season and hope for next. Here's the letter to my favorite team.

Dear Falcons,

I'm sorry for not watching that last game. I could have helped you win. Sometimes you forget how much your team's success is dependent on me, a mother of four kids. I love bratwurst with grilled onions, but I don't drink beer. I have a tendency to complain using lines from Shakespeare. I don't have many skills in the world, but helping you win is one of

123

them. When I focus. When I try.

Admittedly, the last Falcon's jersey I owned was Deion Sanders #21 jersey. While everybody else is hashtag #RiseUp, I'm still doing the Dirty Bird dance. I have some catching up to do.

Years ago, I wrote a college essay about my future. That essay included a prediction that the Falcons would go to the Super Bowl in 1999. My dream came true. I was wearing my Neon Deion jersey during the playoff game against the Vikings. Sometimes when it is very quiet, I can still hear my echoing screams as Morten Andersen kicked a game winning field goal.

We might not have won the Super Bowl, but I stand by that season. Whenever we lose, I know we can win the next time. By "we," I mean the Falcons and me.

Over the years, I've had kids. I have not been the fan I should be. I committed the worst crime against humanity by marrying a Cowboys fan. We have more than once entered the Dome with me in a Falcon's t-shirt and my husband in an Emmitt Smith jersey. Those are the days I wish I still had my Deion Sanders jersey.

I have failed my team in so many ways. I do watch the game. I don't watch the game. I focus too much on the game. Other times I'm distracted. I never ever pray for a win. That's silly. God's ears are so full up on Sunday, I don't even bother. I need a new lucky Falcon's jersey.

My husband says I don't even know who the Falcon's quarterback is these days. I don't know who the head coach is. I don't. I don't have the capacity to store the starting lineup in my memory anymore. Despite this, I am still a fan. If you are a fan, you've just got to be a fan forever.

For the San Francisco years, I tried to have a second team. It was tough. I could have cheered for the 49ers or the Raiders, but there was always that Cowboy at my side. So I stayed true to the Falcons and apologized to them at the end of every season.

I decided to pick the Colts for my backup team and that

did not turn out so well. How can a quarterback named Andrew Luck not be lucky? Maybe I'm the bad luck.

I might not be superstitious, but I'm optimistic. I'll watch the Super Bowl. I will do the Dirty Bird during the halftime show. But no matter who is on the field, I'll be cheering for the Falcons. When next season starts, I'll be hopeful for wins and free tickets to games. I might not be a lucky fan, but I'm faithful. And I'm going to stay that way.

Next year the Super Bowl.

BALLS, LIES AND LEFT TURNS

It is nice to see the word "balls" in the news. Balls are funny. Deflated balls are extra funny. Thanks to the New England Patriots and the deflated ball scandal of 2015, I giggled quite a bit. Then I got serious. Balls are funny, but cheating is not.

Each morning I drop my kids off at school and notice signs that say "No Left Turn" between 7-8am and 2-3pm, the hours when you drop off or pick up your kids from school.

No matter where I'm going, I always need to make the left turn. My work is left. My house is left. The coffee shop is to the left. Yet every day I turn right. The sign says "No Left Turn" so I turn right. And every morning I watch parents make the left. They are cheaters. If given the chance they would deflate their footballs just to get the advantage over the rest of people who do follow the rules.

There are two types of people in the world. The people who do wrong and know it's wrong. They don't care about the rules. Then there are the people who think the rules don't apply to them. Group one might be criminals, but I'd rather be with them. The people in the second group think that they are above the law.

I make a mental note of the parents who make the left turn.

"No, son. You can't have a playdate with Little Johnny. I've seen his parents make the left turn during right turn only hours. They can't be trusted."

I remember watching my mother in a department store as a child. The clerk had given back too much change. To my child's mind, if someone hands you $100 when you should have gotten $10, the extra money is yours.

"It's stealing," my mom said. The employee was very thankful, and I remained confused. It wasn't the employee's money. Why did it matter?

"She could lose her job over a mistake like that. If the money doesn't add up at the end of the day, even if it's a mistake, she could be fired. It would be lying and stealing to take the money." This is why I needed parental guidance. Finders keepers, losers weepers is a strategy of convenience even for adults.

I am no paragon of virtue. Once over dinner, a friend posed a question, "Do you ever lie?" He claimed to always speak the direct truth. I believe him. If I wear an unflattering dress, this friend might say so. He has a great vocabulary, and I think this affords him the luxury of honesty.

When they got to me, I also told the truth.

"I lie all the time," I said.

I struggle with this. I would never lie at work. When I'm sick I'm sick. If I want to go to a baseball game, I say that. I value honesty, but still I admit to lying. To my kids.

My honest friend is child-free. Honesty is just like breathing to him. For me, I try to be honest. I've struggled with the Tooth Fairy. I waver between moments of truth and allowing magic.

We don't say much about Santa Claus either way, but on the nights when homework is not being done, St. Nickolas rears his ugly head, and I shout. "Santa can see you." No he can't.

There are the lies of hyperbole. "You're going to freeze to death." We live in Georgia. This is unlikely.

And the lies of avoidance. "How babies are made? Well,

there's a penis and a vagina. Sometimes just sperm and egg in a test tube . . . and then a lot of hugging." That's the precursor to the truth.

Which brings me back to #deflategate and football. I think about that guy making the left turn. We are all guilty of excusing our bad behavior. What happens when we live like we are all above the law? Our kids are watching. Will they do what we do?

Is lying about Santa Claus the same as cheating? I don't know. Is cheating worse than making the left turn when no one is looking? I don't know. Is it okay just because it's less wrong than another broken rule?

Now I say, "When you don't put on a coat, you cough, and when you cough you get sick." I'm less hyperbole. I bought a book that explains the part after the hugging. I'm finding ways to be direct and truthful even when I'd rather avoid it.

Leave it to the New England Patriots to ruin something funny like the word balls. Thanks to the Pats I've been in a moral quandary. As for the Super Bowl. Inside I'm still cheering on the Falcons, but outside I'll be shouting "Go Seahawks!" That's the truth.

THE POX

A boy who lived down the street from us had the chicken pox three times. I know this with certainty because we were in the same grade. I knew him all three times he was sick. Even as I think back on it, it sounds like an urban legend. No one had the chicken pox twice. No one had it three times, and that third time was in high school. He was a special case.

Without studying epidemiology or infectious disease, I knew this kid was an outlier. He was not like us. I don't recall him being sickly in any other way. Chicken pox was his thing.

I had chicken pox once. That was enough. I was about four years old, so I mostly remember the stories told to me. My sisters had chicken pox first, and I didn't get sick with them. My immune system held out for almost a year.

"I have the *chivers*," I told my mom. I was roasting with a fever and could not properly describe my chills and shivers. But my mom knew. She'd seen it before.

She put socks on my hands to prevent the scratching. I was small and nimble and itchy. I found ways to scratch. One of the two scars on my face came from the chicken pox. I had to get the itchy bumps off me. I was willing to hurt myself in an attempt to find relief.

If you've had the pox or the measles then you know that moment of insanity when the itchy feeling is in your brain. I do remember that.

Thankfully, I survived with only a few marks to show for it.

Until I had kids, I did not realize that there had been advances in childhood immunizations. I was excited to hear about the chicken pox vaccine. I knew I wanted to spare my kids being sick. I also knew that vaccines were not foolproof. I remembered that kid from my neighborhood. Anyone can be an outlier.

I shop at a local health food store regularly. Once when I was noticeably pregnant, a customer accosted me.

"You shouldn't vaccinate your baby," the lady said. "It's dangerous. Toxic. Your kids will develop autism," she said. She was ruining my normally happy experience.

Never stand between a pregnant lady and the cooked beets on the hot bar.

I smiled. "Chances are good that my children will need to go to school one day. And I don't want them to die."

This was eleven years ago just a mile away from the CDC. I had no idea there was an anti-vaccination movement beginning just at the time I was starting to have kids.

The lady backed away from me and the beets. She had no response for, "I don't want my kids to die." I've only had to use that response a couple of times since.

If you've ever had chicken pox, you don't want your child to have chicken pox. If you're like me, until recently, I never knew a single person who had the measles. Not one. I'm 40. The measles and polio and small pox were diseases of the past.

I'm okay with my kids not having the chicken pox. I remember the *South Park* episode about chicken pox. My mom was disappointed that I didn't get the chicken pox at the same time as my sisters. Exposure was the first vaccine.

I have chicken pox scars on my face. I read Albert Camus's *The Plague*. In college, I wrote a wonderful paper on the bubonic epidemic. *The Walking Dead* is currently my favorite TV show. Things that are contagious fascinate me in history books and in fiction. Not in the news.

I don't expect science to be perfect. There is no exact remedy for cancer or pneumonia or even the measles. Science improves our chances. I'm willing to take a risk for the reduction in risk.

It's the reason I periodically exercise. I'm not trying to wear a bikini or live longer. I want to live better and reduce my risks of becoming sick in preventable ways. Preventable. Living better doesn't mean you won't die. We are all going to die. I'll be a little pissed off if it's the measles that kills me.

ENOUGH SHADES OF GREY

No one has ever stopped me in the grocery store to ask if I've read *Cloud Atlas* by David Mitchell. I have. No one has ever asked me if I've read *The Canterbury Tales* by Geoffrey Chaucer . . . in Middle English. I have. No one cares that I enjoy short stories by J. California Cooper or ZZ Packer. I do. But once a week, in an airplane, on the playground, or at the grocery store, someone stops me to ask me about *Fifty Shades of Grey* by E.L. James.

I did read it, but what you really want to know is if I liked the book for its mysterious hero, romance, and spanky sex. You want to know if this book improved my sex life and marriage.

Or you want to know if I hated the book for its ridiculous plot, implausible characters, and spanky sex. You want to know if the book ended up in a bonfire in my backyard.

I am judgmental. If you make the left turn during "No Left Turn" hours at the school parking lot, I will make a note of it in my Little Book of Human Failings. But I will not judge you for your thoughts on *Fifty Shades of Grey*. Honestly, I don't care enough either way to love it or hate it.

I read it. It was a bit like making my eyes take medicine, but soon enough I finished it. When people ask me about the book, and now the movie, I say the same thing.

"It wasn't the right book for me, but then again neither was David Mitchell's *Cloud Atlas*." If you want to make a stranger go away who insists on talking about kink and BDSM in the grocery store, mention *Cloud Atlas.*

I love the romance genre. I have read a book or two with sex in it. Just because *Fifty Shades of Grey* has "romance" and sex doesn't mean I'm going to like it. Here's the quickie version of the plot:

Billionaire asks virgin to sign a contract so he can tie her up and have sex with her to cure his unresolved childhood issues.

My first issue with the book is about the theme. His unresolved issues include his birth mother, his adopted mother, and his mother's friend. Ewww. As soon as I see the word "mother" in a sexy book, my lady parts shrivel up and die. I'm sure Freud would have been a fan *Fifty Shades*, but not me.

My second issue with the book has less to do with the book and more to do with my life. I'm in that life phase that is exhausting. I analyze, audit, and strategic plan. I spend time in distant cities. My house is a mess. My kids are small. We soccer, ballet, and piano. I fight laundry the way Batman fights crime.

At the end of my work day, the last thing I want to read about is Christian Grey in a tuxedo holding handcuffs. I don't care how rich he is. I turn into my true Jamaican self, grab the nearest wooden spoon, and beat his behind into next week. There is nothing kinky or sexy about it. I feel abused enough during daylight hours. I don't need more when I read.

I have many dear friends who loved the book and will likely spend Valentine's Day watching the movie. This makes me happy. Although the book wasn't for me, I know the joy of loving a book so much that you have to read it over and over again.

I don't believe that those who liked *Fifty Shades* must go find "better" books to read. I love sharing a good book, but it isn't my job to take your good book out of your hands.

Other people can speak with authority about the controversial aspects of the book. I am not an authority on anything other than storyline and romance. I like other novels. I give credit to E. L. James for doing something daring. She put words on a page. It doesn't get more naked than that.

But there's the line in the book where the author lost me forever. Christian Grey says to Anastasia Steele, "I'm going to f— your mouth." What? No. No, you aren't. You don't get to speak that way, even in fiction. I'd rather do laundry. Bye, Mr. Grey.

What kind of kink do I like? Here are three of my favorite love scenes from movies:

Crouching Tiger, Hidden Dragon. Chow Yun-fat and Michelle Yeoh touch hands. That's it. They are fully clothed. They never even kiss. I'm fairly certain that this scene makes people pregnant.

The Terminator. It's not the "Come with me if you want to live" scene but the "I came back through time for you Sarah Connor." Time travel is sexy. Do that, and I might let you spank me.

Star Trek. The rebooted version. Spock is upset and steps into the turbolift and out of nowhere Uhura kisses him. That's the kind of scene that will overheat my warp core. Christian Grey may have unresolved mommy issues, but I've proudly got Vulcan issues.

This proves that you can't trust me on *Fifty Shades of Grey.* For me, less sexy is more. Romance is sweeter and more interesting when it comes from a story not related to romance. For the record, you can have a book with explicit kinky sex and still be nice about it.

Happy Valentine's Day. Get out your silk scarves and feather dusters and whips and handcuffs. I'll be in my wool socks drinking warm milk as I binge watch Colin Firth in *Pride and Prejudice* while snuggling my cat Greg Maddux. I won't judge you for your proclivities, if you don't judge me for mine.

AN OSCAR FOR BILLY ZANE

Every year my sisters and I go to see one Oscar-nominated movie together. We bring our husbands. We debate the films in advance. We each refuse to see some of the movies, and eventually we settle on a movie we all agree on.

I am woefully unaware of current movies and TV shows. This is good because when I go to the movies, I like not knowing about what I'm going to see. Some titles give it away. *Lincoln* or *Twelve Years a Slave*. Okay. I get it. I want to see movies that are interesting and thought-provoking. Possibly happy. Our pick was *Still Alice*. Spoiler alert. It's a cry fest.

They tricked me. At first, the plan was to have coffee with my sisters.

"Let's go to the movies," my oldest sister suggested. Then she mentioned our husbands, and I panicked.

"Is *Still Alice* our Oscar movie?" I asked. I didn't have any Kleenex. I wasn't ready. But I went. I cried. I wiped my two hours' worth of tears on my long sleeves. Thank goodness it's winter.

I love Julianne Moore something awful. She is lovely and accessible. They still owe her an Oscar for her performance in *The Hours*. Another beautiful Oscar-quality movie that I loved

135

and will not see again.

I usually only see one movie a year that is intended for adults. The rest of the time I'm in movies like *Mr. Peabody and Sherman* where my eyes are burned by horrible characters, and my ears are filled with insipid dialogue. I told you *Fifty Shades of Grey* was not for me. No hate there. But I hated *Mr. Peabody and Sherman* with every ounce of my being. There is no word in your language for how much I despise that film. I might not have cried on the outside during that movie, but believe me, I was crying on the inside.

Grown-up movies are supposed to save me, but then why are all Oscar movies so depressing?

Over the years I've seen many Oscar movies with my sisters. *Slumdog Millionaire, Inception, Lincoln, American Hustle, Still Alice*. I had high hopes for *Inception*. It did not make me cry. Handsome actors, mind travel, explosions. It should have been perfect, but it wasn't for me. Damn you, Leo DiCaprio! You lie.

I love seeing movies in the movie theater. I like the darkness and the camaraderie of strangers when the movie elicits a dramatic response from the audience. I like the fact that you can't pause or replay a scene. You just have to catch the action the first time.

I have many favorite movies. Silly movies. Intellectual movies. Foreign films. Why do Oscar movies make me mad? They are always about someone who is dying, mentally or physically challenged, abused, or a prostitute. You can't win an Oscar if you tell a story about happy people.

I encourage you to see *Moonstruck* for my favorite didn't-win-an-Oscar movie. *Moonstruck* is the only romantic comedy I've ever loved. I loved the characters and family dynamics and romance and humor. Maybe I cried a little, but they were happy tears.

I encourage you to see *Zoolander* for my favorite Oscar-didn't-give-this-a-chance movie. I watched *Zoolander* every day for the forty weeks that I was pregnant with my first child. I was morning-sick all day, every day for nine months.

Zoolander saved my life every day.

I can't explain why this specific movie calmed my nightly nausea. It did. It is the only movie I have seen more than two hundred times.

I often speak lines of dialogue from *Zoolander*, forgetting that they don't make sense in the real world.

When my kids argue I'll say, "Listen to your friend Billy Zane, he's a cool dude." My kids don't even know who Billy Zane is. I do. I met him once years ago, and he was a cool dude. Billy Zane has never won an Oscar, but I'd give him one for his brief appearance in *Zoolander*. He made me laugh. He made me smile.

His biography barely mentions *Zoolander* but instead lists movies like *Dead Calm*. I saw that. The title lets you know how happy that movie is going to be. His big Oscar-worthy credit is the movie *Titanic*. You know a movie called *Titanic* is not going to be happy. Thank you Leo DiCaprio for screwing with my mind in *Inception* and *Titanic*.

My sister is a big movie fan who sees everything. *Selma*. *Birdman*. She hardly misses an Oscar picture. Her kids are older. She can do this. After watching *Still Alice*, I turned to her.

"I've been wanting to see *The Imitation Game* with Benedict Cumberbatch. That should be a happy movie," I said.

My sister stared at me blankly. "It's about the war and a scientist who is later persecuted. Excellent movie. Maybe the best movie this year. But I'm not sure that it's happy."

Of course it isn't happy. Oscar movie. What was I thinking? I better get my Kleenex and go see it. I should add a dash of *Selma* when I'm done. Because I will need more crying.

Good thing I like crying.

I hope that Julianne Moore will win an Oscar. Maybe she can dedicate it to my friend Billy Zane. He is a cool dude.

MY ACCEPTANCE SPEECH

I was rummaging through my desk on Monday when I came across a legal pad filled with my dad's handwriting. Each page contained a draft thank you letter to one of his friends.

As you know my surgery was successful, and I am on the road to recovery ... The stitches were removed on Thursday ... Thank you for the fruit basket ... Thanks for the beautiful plant you sent to cheer me up ... Thank you for the prayers, cards, and support.

The handwriting brought my dad back to me for a moment. He was a writer of birthday and Christmas and thank you cards. I'm not. He took time to write thank you notes, not once, but twice. The second time he would write the note in a nice card or on good paper.

I also write longhand, but sometimes it is days or weeks before I put a pen to actual paper. I wonder if I would recognize my own scrawl as easily as I know my father's.

I write one-draft thank you notes. I lack my father's courtesy. If I make a mistake, I scratch it out even if I am writing inside the nice card or on the good paper. My dad was thoughtful. He enjoyed corresponding with people. He made time to write and say thank you.

I did not watch The Academy Awards. I understand that Julianne Moore did not thank Billy Zane when she won. That's all right. I spent Oscar night doing what I always do on Oscar night: I draft my Oscar acceptance speech even though I have no chance of ever winning the award.

I'd like to thank my third grade teacher, Mrs. Lambeth, for calling on me when I raised my hand. Thank you to the stranger who gave me five dollars in cash when the credit card machine was broken at the gas station, and I was completely out of gas. Thank you to all my friends who still accept me when I send my thank you cards two years too late.

There are reasons why I should stay away from microphones. I'm terrible at saying "thank you." I'd forget to thank my fifth grade math teacher, my friends who ran the zombie 5K with me, and the people who sent flowers when my dad passed away.

"You didn't know me before my mother died," one friend said to me as she brought us three dozen bagels. Mourning food. "I used to be so happy."

She and I ran the zombie race together the year before. She couldn't be any more fun. I'm always thankful for zombies and friends who like zombies. But I would probably forget to thank her in my acceptance speech. And I still owe her a thank you card for the bagels.

My Oscar speech is never the same twice. I'd ramble. I'd be both flippant and overly sentimental. There would be laughter and tears. It would be the best Oscar speech ever.

Okay, I'm a dreamer. I prefer life behind a keyboard. I am more precise with a pen. I should stay away from microphones. I should go back to written correspondence.

When J.K. Simmons received his Oscar for best actor in a supporting role, he said, "Call your mom, call your dad. If you're lucky enough to have a parent or two alive on this planet, call them."

On Sunday afternoon, I stood in my mother's kitchen. She told me how hard she worked to get the mud out of my kid's snow gloves.

"Listen to them for as long as they want to talk to you. And thank them," J.K. Simmons advised in his acceptance speech.

My kids spent winter break making mud pies in my mom's backyard. I should thank her for loving us, dirt and all.

In April, I will stand behind a microphone as a part of the Atlanta cast of the *Listen to Your Mother* show. My piece is an Oscar speech of sorts. An acceptance speech. While I know nothing of mothering my own kids, I know a lot about motherhood from watching my mom and being thankful for her.

It makes me wonder what kind of thank you is enough.

My dad's old thank you cards are lost in distant desk drawers and filling up landfills. He said his thanks, and now he's moved on.

I've got a lot of catching up to do. There are so many different people to thank. Better now than in November.

For the bagels and flowers and zombie race. For drinking whiskey with me on the eve of my birthday. For not laughing when I crazy dance. For calming me when I rage. For the mud. For clean gloves. For the legal pad on a Monday morning when I could not call my father.

When I found his handwriting, my dad called me. He told me to write an acceptance speech. He told me to grab the microphone. He told me to say thank you.

VULCAN GREETINGS AND GOODBYES

As I walked through the airport in Washington D.C., a man approached me while making the Vulcan greeting with his hands. This unexpected gesture made me smile, and then laugh.

He stopped in front of me and introduced himself.

"You gave a presentation to my team last month. You mentioned that you loved Mr. Spock in your introduction."

It was true. I carry a Spock doll with me to business meetings. The entire crew of the Starship *Enterprise* sat on my desk. Uhura, Scotty, Bones, and Kirk kept me company. On more than one occasion, I'd walk into the cafeteria at work and someone would give me a Vulcan greeting.

Live long and prosper.

The correct response is "Peace and long life" or you can say "Live long and prosper" back. I have no problem adding a little science fiction to my professional life. If you know me, then you know I like Spock. Thanks to Gene Rodenberry and the universe he created, there will be other Vulcans. I like any iteration of Spock. But there will only be one Leonard Nimoy.

The first time I went to the IMAX Theater in Boston, the voice of Leonard Nimoy pierced the darkness. It sounded like an old friend. I felt a spine tingling nostalgia and sadness that day. This week was not the first time I've cried over Spock.

I wasn't born a *Star Trek* fan. I was raised one. I did not get it from my mom or dad. It was a gift from my two older sisters. When kids my age were playing with Barbie and G.I. Joe, I was working on my Starfleet Academy application. As a future science officer on the *Enterprise*, my sisters knew not to give me baby dolls. They gave me an autographed picture of Nichelle Nichols for my 10th birthday. Because that's what normal 10-year-old-girls got for their birthday.

My sisters were nerds when being a nerd was an insult. I didn't know any better. I was raised on a strict diet of *Buck Rogers* and *Battlestar Galactica*. I never choose between *Star Wars* and *Star Trek* because I equally love both.

Even though I was little, my sisters set the precedent that we would see every *Star Trek* (and *Star Wars*) movie on opening day. When the *The Wrath of Khan* premiered, my parents took us to go see it. My parents weren't into *Star Trek*. Ever. It wasn't their thing, but they indulged us. Your kids can't get into too much trouble if their dearest friends live in galaxies far, far away.

In those days movies were a big deal. You couldn't watch TV and movies on demand or on your phone. You only had one shot at seeing a movie, especially on opening day.

When I was seven years old, I saw *The Wrath of Khan* at Phipps Plaza in Atlanta. We had to wait in line most of the day to get tickets, and then wait again for our showtime. People came prepared with blankets and slept in line. That's how much we loved *Star Trek*.

Even though Ricardo Montalbán was the villain, I thought he was beautiful. Even though Spock was supposed to be Kirk's sidekick, he was always the hero to me. The end of the movie proved I was right: unlikely heroes make the best heroes. I only cried because heroes aren't supposed to die. I wanted to be a Vulcan that day and so many others. It seemed like a superpower to have self-control and logic in a world with none.

Damn it, Jim, I cried a little when Leonard Nimoy died. It

must be something about turning 40, because I cry darn near every week these days. I'm not a Vulcan. None of us will ever be. And that's a shame.

The future isn't about technology and machines. The past isn't about dirt floors and manual labor. The future and the past are about people. That's why I like old Westerns and why I like *Star Trek*. That's also why I'll miss Leonard Nimoy.

Spock made us question our feelings and actions. Why do we resist logic? Why do we love? Spock had the best of both worlds. He was half human and half Vulcan. He would pity us during our mourning and our loss. But he would be reasonable. Sadness is illogical, but it is inevitable.

Many friends consoled me, as though I lost a family member. A friend told me, "He is and will always be your friend." That felt like a Vulcan greeting and goodbye. We had an unlikely hero in Mr. Spock. We had a friend in Mr. Nimoy. Good thing Spock will always be with us.

Peace and long life.

PICKY EATERS

I'm allergic to beef. This is something new to me. I've eaten beef my whole life until I had kids. During my first pregnancy, I only ate beef. It had to be ground beef. That was my *Zoolander* pregnancy. I was sick and could only stomach four things to eat: ground beef, corn, cheddar cheese, and cherry tomatoes. That's it. It was horrible. It's no surprise that my first child is my pickiest eater.

The other pregnancies were no better. With child number two, I only ate Indian food. Specifically palak paneer which is a spicy spinach curry with cheese cubes. That child is my most adventurous eater. With the boy, I ate sushi for breakfast, lunch, and dinner. He loves the water, and he eats like a whale. My last pregnancy was spinach smoothies. She eats, no lie, a pack of seaweed every day for breakfast.

Sometimes I feel like I'm to blame for their picky habits. Dinner time is a Shakespearean tragedy with one child wailing and another child giving a monologue on why she should not be forced to drink apple juice.

That's right apple juice.

My kids had the freshly pressed apple juice at my sister's house a while ago. They all seemed to enjoy it. I decided to buy some as an upgrade from the typical clear apple juice, but when I served it with dinner the gnashing of the teeth started.

"It tastes funny," one said before she ever let it pass her lips.

"It looks weird," another said with tears streaming down her face.

What was happening? This was the "good" apple juice. "Doesn't our regular apple juice look like pee?" I asked.

"No!" they shouted, and then they looked at the regular apple juice. Upon realizing it does look like pee the crying got louder.

"There's stuff in it," the third one said.

"It's apples. The stuff is apples. You eat apples every day," I said. Actually, I shouted this. Because I hadn't served them human heads. It was apple juice.

So I told them the horrible truth.

I told my second child she once picked up and almost ate a Palmetto bug. If you are from the North, you might not realize that "water bug" or "Palmetto bug" are fancy ways of saying cockroach. My daughter was about two when this happened. She picked up a dead bug and almost put it in her mouth, but I did a dive, tuck, and roll to knock it out of her hand.

"You almost ate a cockroach," I said. "Think about that."

She stopped crying.

The boy almost ate a dead field mouse. Back in the days when I only had three kids, I would set them loose in the backyard while I mowed the lawn. He was probably also two at the time. Kids at age two will eat anything. I remembered thinking how sweet he looked sitting in the grass on the far side of the lawn. Then he lifted something from the ground. By. Its. Tail. He raised it into the air and opened his mouth like an alligator. I screamed so loud he tossed the carcass away and started crying. Upon hearing this story, his tears over the apple juice stopped.

"You almost ate a rotting mouse," I said. I smiled at the fresh pressed apple cider.

My oldest, the pickiest eater, looked at me with nervous eyes. She is picky about food and picky about medicine. I can only count twice in her life we've ever been able to pry medicine down her throat.

"I'd rather have the fever," she told me once when I offered her baby Tylenol.

I shook my head at my firstborn. She tends to be sweet natured, but her unbuttered bread and unsalted baked potatoes and unflavored diet often gets on my nerves. In her perfect world, she would eat edamame and rice every meal.

"You ate a small tube of Monistat," I said. Just the thought of that day makes me want to cry. She was probably also two. She liked to pull out the shampoo and soap from under the bathroom cabinet. She'd entertain herself for hours putting our house into disarray. Then it got quiet. Quiet is bad.

My daughter was sucking on a 1 ounce tube of Monistat. I started crying, grabbed her, and called poison control. I still feel the leaden beating of my heart as I waited for someone to answer.

I explained what she ate. I told them I lived near enough the children's hospital and the general hospital. I said I would hang up and call an ambulance. I thought about them pumping her stomach. My first-aid training came back to me. I remember that some poisons should not be regurgitated.

"You don't need to do anything," the lady at poison control said. "It's totally fine to eat Monistat even in larger quantities."

What?

"I should take her to the pediatrician then?" I asked. My tears were replaced by utter shock and confusion.

"No. She'll be fine."

Even though she was fine, I was shaken for weeks. All of our medicines and cleaning supplies were locked up or stored in high cabinets. The only open cabinet was for our shampoo, soap, toilet paper, and Monistat.

"What's Monistat?" my now-10-year-old asked me.

"Not food. Something that made me call poison control. I can't imagine it tasted good, but you ate that," I told her.

"Surely, the good apple juice can't be worse than Monistat."

So they tasted the pressed apple juice while holding their noses. Then they explained that their tears were because my sister had a different brand. I won't tell you what happen the night we sautéed spinach. These kids have that tale of woe thing down to a science. Shakespeare would certainly be proud and hungry.

BECOMING A PRINCESS

No matter how good your fairy godmother is, some of us just aren't made to be princesses. My family was disappointed with my approach to my wedding. I wanted to run away to Las Vegas to get married. I thought a destination wedding to Jamaica would be perfect. Instead, I had a traditional wedding.

We were conservative with our budget. We paid for almost everything in cash. The guest list was limited to 70 people. We didn't have a honeymoon. I wasn't a bridezilla about anything.

I only wanted lots of food and cake. I wanted mojitos and champagne. I let the restaurant pick the dinner menu. I let my florist design the flowers. I had no idea what my bouquet would look like until I got to the church that morning.

The only real decision I had to make was choosing the wedding dress. I've avoided being girly most of my life. I despise shopping. I hated the thought of spending hours looking at dresses. Mojitos are much more fun.

But I had to have a dress. I thought I might like something simple. Something appropriate for my body type. Something pretty. Something neat. The owner of the bridal shop and my sisters indulged me as I picked out dresses. They tried to steer me towards lace and pearls while I looked for the cheapest dress that might look flattering on me.

Eventually the owner said, "You pick the first two dresses. I'll pick the third."

I tried on the first dress. It looked like a white sundress. I tried on the second dress. It looked like a pretty white dress for a cocktail party. Nice, but not spectacular.

Then the owner emerged with his pick. His dress was horrific. Ivory tulle with pink roses and a 10-foot train.

"No way," I said.

"Put it on," he said. He wasn't smiling.

If you have never gone wedding dress shopping, I hope you can avoid this terror. They shove you into the dress in a fitting room sans mirror. The shop owner's henchmen are usually two little ladies from the old country. You pick the country. While admonishing your American fattiness, they zip and cinch and tie you into a white puff ball. You can't see yourself until you march out into the main store and onto a stage for all the other customers to see.

You try to keep your cleavage from falling out of the top of the dress. You try not to trip on the excessive fabric. You try not to be irritated by the teenager from Buckhead whose cotillion dress will cost more than your wedding dress. You try to smile at the pageant kids who are dress shopping in the flower girl section. You try not to think about Vegas and the soft-sand beaches in Negril.

You step on the stage. Put on a fake smile and open your eyes. And then every person in the store burst into tears.

When I looked in the mirror, I saw a princess. Tulle and fluff and cleavage and mini-roses. There was a train and a veil. I felt pretty. I felt shocked. And I loved it. Then I took a closer look at the dress, and it looked like a wedding dress a pirate wench might wear. I loved it even more.

Maybe I needed the chance to be a princess after all.

Now I've got three little princesses of my own. And a little prince. They are each very different.

One is like me. She won't wear dresses. One likes skirts with mismatched knee socks. The boy likes blue jeans all the time. Even for soccer.

Then there's the baby princess.

She put on a fluffy pink dress to go see the movie *Cinderella*. She is four years old. She calls any fancy dress her "wedding dress," but she refused to wear anything resembling glass slippers on her feet. She wore combat boots. She looks dainty at first glance, then you realize that if you give her half a chance she'll stomp the crap out of you.

There is power in dressing up. I spent my college years in combat boots. When you lace up your boots you feel strong, you feel different.

I spent my younger life fearing princess dresses. I used to believe that beauty was the antithesis of intelligence. Femininity the opposite of power. I don't feel that way anymore. The only thing I prize now is comfort. And I also value the opportunity to step out of my comfort zone every once in a while.

I didn't dress up as a child, but as an adult I look for opportunities to play make-believe. I put on my cape. I feel super. I put on my combat boots. I enjoy a twirl in a pretty dress. I believe in magic and change.

Cinderella's first choice for a dress was simple. She would have been happy at the ball in plain shoes and a hand-me-down dress. But she got so much more.

My fairy godmother was a grouchy guy on the other side of Atlanta. He might not have been smiling, but he knew how to make magic.

I wouldn't change anything about my wedding day. My bouquet was perfect, red roses. I had a mojito. I had champagne. My prince did not have a sword or a horse, but he made up for it in jokes. We laughed all day. We smiled all night.

The only thing I might have changed about my wedding would be the shoes. Forget glass slippers. If I had to do it again, I'd be like my daughter. I'd be a princess in combat boots.

RULES FOR KIDS

The best tool you can give a child is a shovel. – Hillary Rodham Clinton
My only job in life is to keep her off the pole. – Chris Rock

You know when you get so angry, you're afraid you'll say something crazy? I was so angry, I was afraid I was about to reveal my true self. That's when other people should be afraid.

There's a kid who's been picking on my child, and I wasn't sure of the best way to handle it. And I almost never handle anything the best way.

First, I told my child to stand up to the other kid. The problem continued.

Second, I alerted the teacher. The problem continued.

Third, I talked to the other child.

I saw the instigator after school one day.

"I hear you've been teasing my kid. Do you think that's nice?" I asked.

The child's face went pale. His eyes got watery. I heard a quiet, "No."

"Well, I expect you to be nice. If I hear that you're saying mean things again, I'd like to talk to you about it. Again. Okay?"

I said this channeling my best Eddie Haskell and Nellie Oleson. Kids today don't know about Eddie and Nellie, but there is something ominous about delivering a message is a sugary-sweet tone. *Yes, Mrs. Cleaver.* I was smiling like Jack Nicholson in *The Shining. All work and no play makes Jack a dull boy.* Talk about crazy.

The instigator agreed to be nice. So far there has been no more teasing.

Everyone has advice for dealing with bullies. Kids need to be confident when challenged by a bully. Kids need to stand up for themselves or their friends when bullied. All the anti-bullying education is for the victims. I wish for once we would focus on the perpetrators and tell them to shut the f*ck up.

That's right. Kids need to be quiet. Kids need to be corrected. Kids don't always know the right thing to do until an adult tells them. Believe me. My kids have been guilty of being jerks, too.

When my daughter was the culprit of hurting her friend's feelings, I gave her some advice.

"You don't have to be friends with everyone, but you have to be nice to everyone. If you can't be nice, go get a book and sit in the corner. That's how I became such a good reader."

Bullies aren't bad kids. They are kids without filters. They are kids without self-control. Sometimes they are kids who need some extra space. We used to say that kids should be seen and not heard. I agree. The genius who invented the Quiet Game should've won a Nobel Peace Prize.

I don't pretend to be the cool mom. When my kids' friends come over to my house I announce, "This is your audition. Your behavior over the next two hours will determine if you get invited back to this house. You've been warned. I expect you to be nice."

I don't mind if kids are obnoxious or loud or eat all the Nutella in the house. I don't mind running or digging in the dirt or using my good yoga mat for a tea party.

I want my kids to respect other people. No matter the day

of the week, we always seem to walk into Big Kroger as the senior citizen bus arrives. I constantly have to remind my kids not to bulldoze over granny just because she's slow.

I have to remind them to hold the door open for others. This is the South. I don't care about gender equality. When it comes to opening doors, I disproportionately want my son to hold open the doors for ladies. At the same time, I expect my girls to be willing to open the door for boys, too.

My kids are sick of me correcting them. I remind them that if they do what I ask the first time, I won't have to repeat myself. My list of rules for kids grows every day:

Say hello to people when you pass them on the street.

If there aren't enough chairs, give up your seat and allow an adult to sit.

Treat your waiter with respect. Look your server in the eyes and ask her how her day is going.

Don't think any job is beneath you. Maybe you'll need a shovel. Maybe you'll need a toilet bowl brush.

Know when to walk away. Know when to run. I'll attribute that piece of advice to Kenny Rogers.

Learn when to be quiet. Learn when to speak up.

You don't have to be right or first.

I'd rather someone calls you a hard worker or curious. Smart does not always mean diligent.

If life was fair, it wouldn't be fun.

Make friends with kids who help you be a better person.

Kids will be kids. I can deal with mud on the floors and rocks in the laundry. But parents have to parent. That means my kids will have to sweep and fold clothes. Sometimes they do these things with tears streaming down their faces.

I have to stop and hug and kiss them. But I don't dry their eyes. I remind my kids that there are rules for parents, too. Rule number one? Sometimes, kids cry because they know we are right.

TO THE STRIP CLUB

I was at the gas station one day when I witnessed a conversation between two strangers. It was Friday night.

A big burly man approached another man in a business suit and asked, "Do you know how to get to Pin Ups?"

"Pin Ups?" the other guy asked.

"It's a strip club," the big guy explained. "On Ponce."

The second man was not from the neighborhood. He started giving directions downtown and to The Clermont Lounge, Atlanta's most notorious strip club, also on Ponce de Leon Avenue.

"But they said it was around here," the big guy said.

I had to help. It was the polite thing to do. Every once in a while you realize that your Southern hospitality includes giving directions to Pin Ups, the lovely strip club in my neighborhood.

I got out of my car and shouted, "Pin Ups is just down the street. Take a left at the second light, and it will be on your left."

Both men stared at me. Particularly the second guy in the suit. *Did that nerd lady just give better directions to the strip club than me?* Yes, I did.

I guess I know why this looked crazy. Me. Minivan. MILFy. The men were startled because I'm not supposed to

154

know where the strip club is. I'm not supposed to encourage men by giving them directions to the strip club. I could not be the kind of lady who would condone strip clubs.

But what's weirder? Giving the directions to the strip club or not knowing how to get there?

The two men went their separate ways and left me in a quandary. The next time I drove by Pin Ups, I slowed down and took a closer look. I was beginning to compose my rant on our oppressive patriarchal society and the objectification of women. I had a second rant about how I should know about strip clubs and be an advocate for women no matter their profession.

But my rant never occurred, because I noticed something wonderful when I drove by. Pin Ups has the best neighbors ever.

The strip club. The pet crematory. The wholesale Asian grocery store.

We live in a world with a lot of division. We separate ourselves based on race or politics or social status or gender. I'm always hopeful. I wonder about the way the world could be or should be. Sometimes I need a reminder that we can all be living in harmony.

As I drove by, I imagined that the owners of each business are friendly with each other. That the three of them get together regularly to talk business and share marketing techniques.

I don't imagine that they argue over the recycling bins or parking on Friday night. Only one of the businesses should be busy on Friday night.

I love when I spot coexisting things that don't belong together. The good sesame sauce, sad puppies, and strip clubs. That's harmony.

I've been to a strip club before. I've seen naked ladies dancing. Remember that one time after college when my friends thought it would be funny to go? They paid extra for me to get a lap dance, because me being grossly uncomfortable is worth top dollar.

The stripper looked like Barbie in a kilt. Maybe it was a school girl outfit. She felt sorry for me and even said so as she kissed my cheek. I imagined she was putting herself through medical school and added that she was a feminist studies major. I attributed very academic careers to all the ladies just so I could survive the night.

"Do you think she likes *Star Trek*?" I asked one of the guys in my group. Well, my friends never invited me back to another strip club again.

I've seen naked men dancing. It is weirdly like watching mimes. This was for a girlfriend's bachelorette party in Los Angeles. I might not like naked men, but I really (really, really) like dancing men. I guess my own sexism kicked. They were so greased up I could not attribute any alternate intellectual careers to my naked dance men. I almost had fun that night. I safely avoided any lap dances from my Magic Mikes. Now every time I hear Michael Jackson's "Smooth Criminal" I imagine a man in rip-away pants. Woe is me.

I'm not the right lady to ask about strip clubs unless you need directions. You can't trust my opinion. Just like *Fifty Shades of Grey*, strip clubs are not for me.

Though I haven't been inside Pin Ups, I secretly love to drive past and wonder about the people who work inside. I wonder about the friendly neighboring business.

I can't spend my life trying to right the world. I don't know what is right for everyone.

One day I might need the good sesame sauce. One day I might have to make tough decisions about my pet. My cat Greg Maddux is twelve years old. I write novels with suspense and romance. One day going into a strip club might be required in the name of research for a book.

That burly guy was embarrassed to get directions to the strip club from a soccer mom. That's the real shame. If you are going to go to the strip club, go. Go proud. The fact that he was embarrassed suggests that even he thinks it's a bit wrong. Those are his issues, not mine.

I don't worry about it. What a strange funny world. I

know how to get to the strip club and other places, too. On a good day, I can give you directions to anywhere you want to go.

BUN IN THE OVEN

I went to two baby showers this month Two. I need to do a better job of screening my friends.

A lot of people mistakenly believe that just because I have four kids, it means that I like kids. I don't. Well, I like my own kids. Sometimes I like my nieces and nephews. But generally, I don't like kids. Or other parents.

I support the child-free revolution. All these rich geniuses who purposely avoid having kids. Wonderful for them. I wouldn't wish parenthood on my worst enemy. It's like tasting spoilt milk and having your friend try it.

Some people should not have kids. Not because they are mean jerks, but because parenthood is not for everyone.

I'm one of three girls. A trio of girls is awesome like *Charlie's Angels* or Laura Ingalls and her sisters on the prairie. I always had to be Carrie. The sister with no lines.

I never wanted to be a mom. I have ten different stories about how I came to be a mom. They are all mostly true.

When I was twenty, a psychic in Venice Beach, California told me that I would have three sons. I am proof that he was not a psychic at all. I have a son and three daughters. It would have been nice if the psychic had at least prepared me for life as a mother.

I thought that as a tomboy mom, I'd be the perfect

mother of boys. I like snakes. I like spiders. I know how to catch fireflies and gently roll rolly-pollies.

When my son was about eighteen months old, he got in the one bathroom cabinet that we keep unlocked. I'd removed the Monistat by then and figured it was safe enough for him to pull out the soap and shampoo and toilet paper. Then he got dangerously quiet. When I found him, he was sitting on the floor with twenty-four unwrapped tampons.

My boy peered into the narrow end. He smiled at me with joy in his face and the tampon string dangling before his eye.

"Mommy, I pirate," he said.

I stepped over him. I thought of 30 years in the future when he'd make a splendid husband, not at all phased by the sanitary products hiding under the bathroom sink.

"No, honey. You gynecologist," I said.

When he graduates from medical school, I will tell him this story.

His sister is responsible for all the rocks I wash. She's nine, but her pockets are always full of granite and quartz. I have pulled out leaves and wood chips out of the dryer.

I've had a twenty minute conversation about a stick. The stick that is very special to my child. The stick I will not allow in my house.

I never ever encourage child-free people to have kids. They are better rested. They read more books. They are superior to me.

But their excuses are tired, "I would be a terrible mom." Newsflash: we are all terrible moms.

"I need time for my career," another says.

"Me, too," I say while balancing spinning plates on my head.

We all want the same things. The presence or absence of kids should not be a hindrance to finding satisfaction in life.

At baby showers, I give the same creepy advice in every memory book.

"Trust no one." Usually some stately matron looks at me unhappily for ruining the sacred baby shower with lines from the *X-Files*. Then I amend my advice to "There is no try, just do." *Star Wars* is just a little more palatable.

There was the one time I hosted a baby shower. The theme was the movie *Alien* starring Sigourney Weaver. The invites had an image of the alien pod opening with the green goo oozing down the sides. The tagline was, "In space, no one can hear you scream. Same for the delivery room."

We had alien decorations and green streamers and party plates. It was a co-ed baby shower, and the men were happy to attend a gestational celebration sans pink bows and boys in seersucker suits. Parenthood should be fun, not torture.

I'd like for those high intellectual child-free people to admit that they choose not to have kids because it wouldn't be fun for them. That's okay. I love that reason. Be thankful that you will never be pooped, peed, and puked on at the same time. Be thankful that your tampons have not been used as a telescope. Parenting isn't fun for everyone. It is fun for me.

This is my wish for my child bearing friends. To my friends who are expecting. To my friends with new babies. Trust no one, but yourself. However much fun your kids are going to have, make sure that you have a little more.

A PERFECTLY FUN SNOW DAY IN ATLANTA

Get some beach blankets. The ones you use when you go to Hilton Head. Those are the ones. Giant pink flamingo and the other one with the Atlanta Falcons on it. Put them down in front of any doors where your child might exit and enter covered in snow. If this is the only step you do, you're good.

Go looking for the gloves. Hmm. Those gloves from the Target $1 bin do not look like they will cut it in snow. Put $1 gloves on your kid, then cover those gloves with latex gloves. Check under the kitchen sink.

Remember you bought real snow gloves that one time. Go hunting for them in closets, garage, open the trunk of your mini-van. There is a glove. Wait, there are the swim goggles too. Thought you lost those at the neighborhood pool. Whew. Take out both the glove and goggles.

Realize glove does not have a match. We are in Georgia. We do not need matching gloves. We remind our kids to wear hats and gloves to school. At first opportunity hat gets thrown into a ditch and gloves get thrown down the storm drain. Be thankful for the single glove.

Start adding layers. Much like the order of species (kingdom, phylum, class, order, family, genus, species), we must follow the order of apparel. Tights, leggings, jeggings, stretchy jeans, sweat pants. Then a single long sleeve shirt

161

followed by every soccer jersey your kid has ever worn. This is Georgia. Your child has played at least two seasons of soccer. These jerseys seem water resistant, much like a ski bib.

Remember you own a ski bib from those trips to Lake Tahoe in college. Wonder for a moment if there's a way to shove your 3 year old into it.

Put on the swim goggles. Apply every knit cap and scarf you can find. Zip kids into their jackets. Pull on single glove and latex kitchen glove if needed. Send kids into snow.

Stand at door for 3 minutes. Because that's how long they will stay outside.

Next time advise kids that snow is like fire. It burns. Tell them Georgia snow is more dangerous than Northern snow. Ours doesn't stay fluffy. It melts into slush and slush can easily enter boots and latex covered $1 gloves. Slush can infect you and freeze your nethers and outers and everything in between.

Tell them they have to stay outside until it's worth doing the 3 loads of laundry they are wearing. Go back to garage and get creative. Cardboard box. Check. Huge plastic bin and lid. Check, check. Boogie boards for the beach. Sand buckets, shovel, and pails. Triple check.

Let the kids back in after a few hours. They should look a little stung. You may spy a dried tear on their frozen little faces. They better enjoy it now. There is no day two. Atlantans only get one day of snow. Tomorrow it will be ice. Black ice on the streets. White ice that looks like snow. You will slip and bust your behind so hard you'll be knocked back to SnowJam 1982. Be safe Georgia.

BETTER ONE DAY

Sometimes the words of encouragement that we give others are the words we most need to hear.

I go to church every weekday. It is not that I'm overly pious, but my children's daycare happens to be attached to my place of worship. It is a blessing and a curse.

You can imagine the blessings. They are numerous. Loving teachers, caring environment, and happy children.

But the curse is a strange thing. When I haven't gone to church on Sunday, I still have to show up on Monday to drop off my kids. On Monday I am ashamed.

One particular Monday, I was loading three kids into the mini-van when my pastor approached. Before he could speak, I began to apologize by saying, "I know, I know." I wanted to add that I would be at church next Sunday, but instead my pastor put an arm around my shoulder and said, "One day it will be better." With that and a half hug he moved on.

I drove home that day feeling defeated. He was trying to be encouraging, but all I could think was "Which day? Which day will it be better? Work, kids, family, life, laundry, dishes, everything is killing me. When will it be better? August 27? December 1? Which day exactly would things get better?"

With each question I asked, I kept hearing, "It will be better one day" because it sounded different that Monday.

More like a promise. So I decided I would be patient. I would wait for better.

A few weeks later, my pastor stepped down from his position. I was profoundly sad at the news, and my mind returned to our last brief conversation. "One day it will get better." Those words were given to me after a busy day at work. My kids were tired and restless in the hot car. Those words were said to me like a promise, and I suddenly wanted to give those words back to my pastor.

My favorite Bible verse is Joshua 1:9. It was my favorite when I was a child, and it's still my favorite today. Probably because I am most prone to feeling discouraged that I cling to it. But recently I think about it differently. I have decided two things:

One, I am finished waiting for better. Better is now even with the meowing cat, crying kids, dirty dishes in the sink, and so much to do.

Two, the words of encouragement that we say to others one day might be the words we most need to hear on another. They might be reflected back on us, even subconsciously, so that we can make tough decisions and allow "better" to happen.

While it is easy to give encouragement sometimes it is difficult to hear the words back when we need them. People of faith aren't "believers," but "knowers" and we shouldn't be "waiters," but "doers."

Are you waiting for a better day? Maybe it is today.

GOOD FENCES

I've always loved the line from Robert Frost, "Good fences make good neighbors," even though I disagree with it. I disagree with Frost and love him all the time. I don't take the road less traveled. I take the well-worn path proudly. The road less traveled is less traveled for a reason. That's the road where the path is narrow and tree roots will trip you and there's a mudslide and usually zombies. I'm known for taking the safe path. I don't take Frost's advice about which road to take or the benefit of fences. I'm known for not liking fences.

I have a fence. It is supposed to keep out the coyotes and possibly stray dogs. It is supposed to keep in my children, our hula hoops, and my abandoned vegetable garden. My guess is that my fence also keeps out good neighbors.

I have neighbors on three sides of our fence, but I don't know them all. One neighbor brought us baked goods the week we moved in. We wave hello at intersections. We chat in the coffee shop. But we almost never speak when we are home.

There were only two reasons to have a fence when I was a kid. Swimming pool or dog. If you didn't have a pool or a dog, you didn't need a fence. I grew up without boundaries. I was required to stay within the limits of our yard, but without a fence my backyard seemed endless.

Not so anymore. The reason we chose our house was for the backyard. It is big by city standards, but three times smaller than the one of my youth. I still love it. Sometimes when I am enjoying the pollen-heavy air, I don't see the yard. I see the border. I don't notice the trees and fighting grass. Here Bermuda and there fescue. I see a fence. I wonder what is on the other side.

On my daughter's birthday it grew strangely warm for December. and I wrote this:

It was the kind of December in Georgia where kids shed their jackets, then shed their long sleeves. The day when ladies turned their faces to the sun and after a few moments, grew hot and eventually had to find shade. The men cooked like it was summer. We called to our neighbors over the fences. The one whose daughter floated bubbles toward our noise walked over and got a piece of cake. There are leaves on the kitchen floor. There is icing in the back garden.

I felt strange shouting over the fence that day. I wondered if I was being intrusive to call out and invite my neighbors over for cake. But when they walked over I was immeasurably happy. They had not been in our house before, but we have talked over the fence before. Not often. Like our other neighbors we are more likely to speak when we are not at home. Strange fences.

When everyone else rails against technology and social media, I disagree. Technology was created to dig under and climb over fences like a bad neighborhood cat.

We communicate differently now.

I have carried a single mango to a friend around the corner.

I have seen the village rise up when I have needed strange things like a bow. Did I need a cross bow? Or a hunting bow? Or a bow that a Disney Princess would carry? The next day at daycare a dad walked in carrying a bow for me to borrow. It was as though I had asked for a cup of sugar while shouting from porch to porch.

When my cousin visited from England, I asked my virtual

neighbors for a guitar that he could use. Did I need an acoustic or electric? Did I need a bass guitar? With an amp? The next day I met my neighbor from the East Atlanta Village who brought the guitar to Decatur for us.

I have shoved a ballet leotard and tights in my mailbox for another neighbor to use.

I've loaned out a stroller. I once borrowed a baby gate from a friend for another friend to use for her cat. Our neighborly spirit lives on in a different way.

Something there is that doesn't love a wall,
That sends the frozen-ground-swell under it,
And spills the upper boulders in the sun;
And makes gaps even two can pass abreast.
– Robert Frost

I am that something that doesn't love a wall. I must be the thing that causes our wooden fence to rotten and welcome moss. There is a broken spot where the bad neighborhood cat finds and sleeps among my neglected rows of parsley and cilantro. I don't shoo the cat away. She reminds me that it isn't about the fences. Good neighbors make good neighbors.

A SIMPLE QUESTION

My daughter curled up in bed beside me to do her nightly reading. She's in fifth grade. She's the oldest. I try to enjoy these moments with her, because more experienced parents warn me that her sweetness won't last. One day, she will be spoiled like a rotten piece of fruit. One day, she will despise me. One day, I will embarrass her. One day, she will change.

For now, she is the one most likely to comfort me with a hug. She has my awkwardness and optimism. To her the world is a good place. Her friends are all different, and she loves them. I don't want her to change.

She's been reading a book called *The Boy in the Striped Pyjamas*. It's a book I don't know. Her class is studying World War II and the Holocaust. The book I read at her age was *The Diary of Anne Frank*. The terribleness of the war was looming, but distant.

"During the Holocaust, what happened to the babies?" she asked.

She has reached a double digit age, and yet she is still my baby. I stopped typing and put an arm around her. I wanted to cement my presence next to her even though I know I can't, I shouldn't, keep her my baby forever.

Part of her homework was to make propaganda posters for leaders on both sides of the war. She is supposed to learn what happened and how.

"Do you know what they did to the adults during the Holocaust?" I asked. "What happened to the other Jewish people?"

She knew a lot more than I'd like for her to know at this age.

"They did terrible things," she said. She leaned against me as her mind pieced together starvation and the gas chamber. There were countless other atrocities.

"But what about the babies?" she whispered.

I didn't respond. Most days I think I'm passable as a parent because I don't need quiet, order, or control. I like to laugh. I try to be flexible. I yell to my son, "Go straight up to bed." He responds, "Can I zig-zag?" And I laugh in return and say, "Yes." When my kids are being unruly, I discipline them. Parenting should always be that simple.

She asked again about the babies. My optimism, my skin, my hope are stripped away from me.

"They killed the babies," I said.

This was a terrible bedtime story for a fifth grader. We sat for a long time in uncomfortable silence. She hugged me as she thought about the babies who died. Maybe she was thinking about the mothers, too.

My daughter has seen me cry a lot this year. I have cried more this year than I have all my years combined. She knows it is a new part of who I am, but part of me despises the tears. I hate that I have to explain terrible things to her.

Would I have had to drink out of the colored water fountain? What happened to the babies during the Holocaust? Why did Papa die?

She has to learn eventually, but why now? Suddenly talking about puberty and sex seems so trivial.

Last year, I was chosen to participate in the Glass Leadership Institute, a program through the Anti-Defamation League (ADL). The primary mission of ADL is to stop the defamation of Jewish people and to secure justice and fair treatment for all.

In a world where labels matter, I do not belong with ADL. I'm not Jewish. I'm not an activist of any kind. When my daughter looked at me with tears in her eyes, I wished I was a better authority on the Holocaust and civil rights.

We live in a world where labels matter to some people. Then I remembered that labels do not matter in my house. Not with my kids. I remembered that being an authority involves a willingness to learn and a willingness to act.

I remember that when she sees me cry, she is reminded that it is okay if she does the same.

I say, "Whenever you learn about history. Whenever you watch the news today. Remember that there are countless people working to be kind, working to fight hate, working to help people."

Combating hate, civil rights, and education are some of the pillars of ADL. I can easily rally behind anti-bully campaigns. I have young kids. I support the efforts to protect religious freedom for all people. Faith has been an important part of my life.

I spent a year learning about a variety of topics with the ADL. Some uncomfortable, some uplifting. I heard reminders that for every evil in the world, someone is working to do good.

I will not bring up the Holocaust with my daughter again unless she does. I know we are both changed a little because of her simple question.

I wish I could tell her thank you. Thank you for asking about the babies. Thank you for caring about the babies you will never know. Thank you thinking about the boys and the fathers and mothers and girls like you writing stories in an attic. Thank you for not putting labels on your friends. It does matter. That part of you never has to change.

A WALK IN BALTIMORE

I needed a power strip and extension cord. Nothing fancy. The kind that you could easily find at a local drug store. I was in Baltimore at the convention center. It was April. The end of winter. Still cold, but the sky was blue like spring was coming. I needed directions to the store.

I asked a hotel employee which way to go. The store was five blocks away.

"You can't go out there," the man said. He was pushing a cart with long fluorescent light bulbs. He was an old man. White. He shook his head at me.

It was Saturday morning around 10 am. I was wearing business clothes. A dress and comfortable shoes. It was 35 degrees outside. My winter coat was neon pink.

I pointed to my phone. "This says CVS is down the street," I said. I can walk five blocks in any kind of weather.

"Do you have a gun?" he asked.

I laughed and shook my head. He didn't smile. He was serious.

"You cannot go out there," he added. Blue sky. Beautiful new hotel near the baseball stadium and the convention center. He pointed to the empty streets like the world had come to an end. "They'll kill you out there."

I love zombies. It's my thing. I looked at all the crisp clear sky and new buildings wondered who "they" were. Why couldn't I go outside?

He called out to his colleague, a tall young man in his early twenties. Maybe still a teenager. Black.

"This lady wants to go out there by herself. Tell her."

The kid shook his head at me. "No. You can't go out there. What do you need? Is it an emergency?"

I felt small then. These men shaking their heads at me like I was crazy. "I need a power strip. We need one for the booth in the convention center."

The kid said, "We can get you one. Come with us."

The old white guy and the young black guy led me to a service entrance. I felt a moment of hesitation. They'd just spent five minutes putting the fear of God in me, then led me to a dark hallway.

The older guy knew I didn't have a gun. He shook his head at me again. "It's okay. Where you from?"

"Atlanta," I say. I know a lot about Southern hospitality. But I experienced something different in Baltimore.

I'd never seen the inner workings of a really large hotel before. We walked through a maze of hallways and elevators and stairs. We passed ladies pushing housekeeping carts.

"That's the dining hall." We go by a cafeteria big enough for a high school or hospital.

"Those are sleeping quarters." We passed rooms like college dorms.

There were supplies and storage rooms and offices. At the back of everything was maintenance and the audio visual department.

"This is AV. We have everything."

The young guy brought out a brand new power strip with extension cord still in a box.

"I'll bring it back on Tuesday," I said, but they told me to keep it.

"Just don't go out alone," the older guy said. He walked away while I tried to profusely thank him. He couldn't care less about my thanks. He made the kid walk me back to the lobby, because there was no way I'd find my way back alone.

I turned my thanks to the kid, but he was the same as the old guy. He didn't want to hear it. Both men refused to give me their names. I ask about Baltimore.

"You'll get robbed over here. Especially looking like a tourist."

I love my neon pink coat. I look like a tourist when I'm at home, too. I tell the kid this and he laughed. When people won't accept your thanks, give them a smile instead. He left me in the lobby feeling thankful.

I like to get out into the cities where I travel. I hate being cooped up inside. Recycled air and fluorescent lighting don't agree with me.

When I was in New York, the bellman told me I couldn't walk to my meeting. "Where are you from?" he asked. Somehow Atlanta suggests an SUV suburban life. People assume I'm ill-suited for the big city. I explained that I drive a mini-van, I've never seen an episode of Real Housewives of Atlanta, and I live in town. The bellman still doubted me.

I walked the twenty blocks to my meeting in New York with no problem. Business dress. Comfy shoes.

When I was in downtown Philadelphia, the bellman told me I couldn't walk to the campus of the University of Pennsylvania because it was two miles away. I can walk two miles. I did walk two miles. No problem.

When I was in Baltimore, I spent all my time inside. I followed the catwalks that connected the hotel to the convention center. I looked at the harbor from behind glass. It wasn't like me, but I never felt afraid of Baltimore for one second.

Those two men were trying to protect me. Could be they were right. Could be they underestimated me. Either way, they gave me kindness.

I didn't walk in Baltimore. But I got a glimpse of the city.

They gave me a glimpse of all the working people in a city that no one sees. The people who cook and clean and fix the lights. The ones who walked me through the maze. No one will tell you about them.

REMEMBER YOUR MOTHER

When my dad died, we forgot about my mother. We remembered her in those silly ways. Meals, when food tasted like nothing. Company, when the echoing silence of his absence became too much to bear. We remembered to feed her, to be with her, but mostly she was forgotten.

It took me an entire year to figure out that honoring the memory of my dad meant honoring the presence of my mom. That's the way people are. We think about the things we don't have. We enjoy memory because it is false. That's the way I am.

When my dad died, I began thinking about my parents as people. "Mom" is a job and a title. My mom was the girl who was a spitfire. My mom was the girl who loved horses. The girl who mourned her pet chickens and refused to eat meat. My mom was not always a mom. I needed this year to remember that.

I walked onto a stage and told a story about my mom and about me becoming a mother as part of the *Listen to Your Mother* show in Atlanta.

I wanted to talk a little about how you become a mother even though it is something I can't explain. There are very few days when I feel like a mother. I'm still a girl who likes Westerns and magic. I have a vivid imagination, but I felt afraid to tell my story. I felt more like a child than a mother. As I prepared to take the stage, I learned a little about being born.

The wings of the stage are dark. There are terms for each side of the stage and the stage curtains. Not right and left or curtain. Foreign words. It was like being on a ship. Enter on the port side. Exit starboard. There was a moment of listing, when the stage gently moved from side to side. I'd never been so scared in my life.

In the shadows of the stage, I remembered that my mom and I are the same. She would not want to walk out onto a stage in front of an audience. I was about to reveal her secrets and mine. Secrets about those who have lost their mothers and their babies. Those who remember fondly and with regret. Those who can laugh and smile. We all can do these things. We share the same secrets.

For a moment, I thought about my father. I looked around the theater for my dad. My dad's death is not so far away for him to feel gone. He walked on stage with me. He made my feeble voice sound strong and true.

He would have like the production of it all. Live microphone. Spotlight. Applause. He would have thought about his own mother, Rose.

My mom thought about her mother, Ethel, who died too young.

My husband thought about his mother and his grandmother. My sisters were there to hold my mom's hand.

Maybe it is easier for me to think about my mom and the mothers who came before me than to think about myself as a mom. All of us together have stories and secrets. With kids and without, with mothers and without.

I walked on stage only worried about what my mom would think. And yet I knew she wouldn't care if I stumbled over my words or if I felt like crying. Of all the people in this world, she had endured most of my tears.

That Saturday night, I was the first to read. I was scared, but then I remembered that the stories after mine would only get better and better until the end. The weight of my anxiety lessened.

We told 13 stories. Thirteen has always been one of my favorite numbers because I don't believe in luck, good or bad. The 13 motherhood stories sounded familiar to me. We were each telling our secrets. One day you find out that all of our secrets are the same.

The story I least expected made me cry. It was the happiest of stories. Life is funny that way. Even happiness can make you sad. Sadness can make you thankful. Thankfulness can make you laugh.

When I left the stage, I never stopped feeling afraid. But I did feel happy. I thought about my grandmothers and their untold stories. If those women were alive to hear our stories today, they would have recognized our words for their truth. For the secrets we normally keep. We write and read to find and share these same secrets over and over again.

We all have stories. We should be afraid of the spotlight and also the shadows. We should remember our mothers. Even the absent ones. Even the ones who made mistakes. We should remember their stories. Someone might need to hear that story. I never knew about the horses. I had to laugh about the chickens. I never thought to ask. But I was glad when she told me.

THE BIG BANANA

I watched my son eating a banana for several minutes, and it took me awhile to realize that something was wrong.

"That's a really big banana," I said.

"No, it's not," he responded.

He is seven years old. What does he know about big bananas? A banana should take you two minutes to eat. He'd been eating for five.

I looked on the counter and saw the rest of the bunch. Sure enough they were all big enough to measure the distance from my widow's peak to my dimpled chin. Those were big bananas.

"Where did Daddy buy the bananas?" I asked.

"The Farmers Market," my son said.

"Well, they are selling GMO bananas at the Farmers Market."

The child, who had no idea when to worry about the size of a banana, knew exactly the meaning of GMOs. I learned about GMOs from my kids. Last week. Needless to say, my son took offense at my GMO comment, delivered at the same time he took his final bite of the gigantic banana.

I wanted to tell him the details of how you become a banana expert. Like being born in Jamaica and eating banana fritters every Saturday of my formative years. Like being 40 years old and married. I've seen my share of bananas in my life. But I spared him the details of my experience.

He won't trust me on bananas. I like my bananas yellow with green stems. Once the entire fruit is yellow, the bananas are too sweet for me. Honestly, I'm allergic to them. If I eat a ripe banana or plantain, my tongue will burn for an hour. My son is my banana opposite. He likes his speckled with brown spots. He will not eat a banana until it is past ripe, almost bad. I wonder what I did wrong to deserve such a strange banana kid.

Brown bananas have their place in my life. Cooked into other things like pancakes and muffins. Even paleo style mushed up with egg or egg and almond meal is pretty darn good. Better yet sautéed with butter and brown sugar. You can't do that with green stem bananas. I'm a banana expert.

I spent the rest of my week hunting for the big bananas. I'm always in a grocery store. I'm not overly brand loyal. I go to the Dekalb Farmers Market and Kroger. I go to the Little Kroger and Big Kroger. Big Kroger is becoming the Really Really Big Kroger. I know a big Kroger when I see one. I know Kroger the same way I know bananas. Years of experience.

I go to Publix and Whole Foods. I have never ever seen a really big banana in Whole Foods. I have also never bought bananas in Whole Foods. I have bought cherries and fresh fish and the good cheese, but never bananas. Probably because the bananas at Whole Foods are extra small. I've got to find a happy medium somewhere.

I go to Trader Joe's when I'm on that side of town. No one is in there for the bananas unless they start shoving bananas in bottles of wine. So I have to rely on my neighborhood grocery stores and the Farmers Market.

My kids have mixed feelings about the Farmers Market. It is bitterly cold inside. So cold that we keep spare coats in the car all summer for unexpected shopping trips. We mark the changing of the seasons by how close the temperature outside matches the temperature inside.

When I was a kid, I had mixed feelings about the same Farmers Market too. It was smaller and at another location down the road. There always seemed to be an inch of gray water on the floor. I would beg my mom not to make me go with her. In those days, she was looking for the bigger bananas and cantaloupe and fish. Now the size of things makes me suspicious.

I still sing the "Let's go Krogering" song from 1980, which means I'm pretty excited for The Really Really Big Kroger. Not that I need one, but I can buy a baby crib at 2 a.m. in the grocery store if I need to. You know how those baby showers sneak up on you.

I'm not as certain about the future home of the new Farmers Market. I've been watching the terraforming of the land each day. I have seen more coyotes, rats, and rabbits in my yard than I have seen in my entire life. There is a new wall holding up the ground that can be seen from outer space. Suddenly the Really Really Big Kroger looks like a botanical garden.

All this, just so I can get big bananas?

I'm not one to boycott places, unless they are places I already don't go. If I looked deeply into the business practice of any business, I would be without any place to shop. I admit I shop everywhere. You can get a half a pound of turmeric for 27 cents at the Farmers Market. Kroger keeps my 2 a.m. shopping habit covered. If Whole Foods dares to open a store in Decatur, let it be known now, I will buy all the good cheese on opening day. I'll still be spotted at Publix. There are those days where I do not have the strength to push my grocery cart to my car.

I needed the bananas to remind me that bigger isn't always better or worse. But it does grab my attention every now and then.

21 PAIRS OF UNDERWEAR

Nobody listens to graduation speeches. I've sat through dozens of them in my life. I've heard Mikhail Gorbachev and Oprah Winfrey. I've heard astronauts and poets laureate speak. It must be tough to stand in front a bunch of optimistic academics and say, "Don't let the door hit you where the good Lord split you."

My niece has graduated from high school. She was my first baby. I'm trying to calmly accept the prom pictures and plans for New York University. But she is going to The New York City, and yes, I say this with a Texas accent.

No one tells you the truth when you go off to college. Your real suitcase needs 21 pairs of underwear. Your figurative suitcase should be equally practical.

1. You will alternate between desperate longing for home and forgetting to call your mom for two weeks.
2. Depression can happen. Sadness. Feeling overwhelmed. Anxiety. Learn to notice when your mood changes and be your own advocate. Eat. Sleep. Exercise. Ask for help. I did. Go see a counselor.
3. It is okay to not become a doctor or lawyer or actor. My sister who wanted to become a lawyer became a lawyer. My sister who wanted an MBA got her MBA. I did not become

a doctor. I thought this was a failure. No one told me it was okay to change my plans. No matter what you become, we all end up watching the same crappy shows on TV. You think AMC or HBO cares what kind of major you were when they decide to rip out your heart? No.

4. Life is fair. We might not have the same opportunities, but we have the same choices. The choices are work hard, work smart, be silent, be silent and listen, listen, ask for help.

5. Life is not fair. You will have some $hitty teachers in your life. This is fine. $hitty teachers are just preparing you for $hitty bosses.

6. You will have far more excellent teachers (or bosses) in your life. Take note of what makes them excellent and emulate that. Also thank them.

7. Remember that you are Southern. You know about football. You are kind. You know a little about zombies. You love God. There are only two things that impress a good Southern girl: Jimmy Carter and golf-ball sized hail.

8. No job is ever beneath you. Now. In college. In the future. You're a vegetarian, but take the job in the cafeteria deboning chicken for a semester. I did this. If you round up all the good people on the planet, at some point they all had the job deboning chicken or shoveling horse poop.

9. Before you kiss anyone, ask yourself if you will be embarrassed to run into this person at Lenox Square Mall in 20 years. Because it will happen. Even if you go to school in California. Even if you go to school in New York.

10. At some point, your weekend meal plan will be Ramen noodles and Halloween candy. This is not acceptable. Consider Cheerios and cheese sticks as a healthy alternative.

11. Keep company with friends who have higher standards than you do. There are bad people in the world. Know this. Avoid the bad ones.

12. You do not have to pull all-nighters. Plan ahead. Go to

bed early, set the alarm for 2 a.m., and write that paper just before class.

13. Put one ridiculous word in every paper you write. Consider these: juggernaut, oyster, unadulterated.

14. Have one fluff sentence in every paper. This one comes from Mr. DiMuro of upstate New York: "When one considers the vast implications of the matter at hand, the prospects stagger the imagination." A little levity may get you a passing grade or reduce your stress just enough to do good work.

15. Take a calculus-based astronomy class even if you are a theater major. Take a painting class even if you are in computer science. Your bag of tricks should be varied. I was an English major, and I can calculate the distance from Earth to Proxima Centauri based on the wavelengths of light. Be a student of everything.

16. In four years, you'll feel the same way about college as you did about high school. Happy you did it. Thankful it is over. You will continue to be excited, happy, and thankful at all the different stages of your life.

17. Don't put deadlines on personal achievements. You never have to get married or have kids or have a specific job. Those things don't follow timelines.

18. Do put deadlines on learning new skills or studying abroad or evolving yourself. You control these things. You can make these things happen.

19. You aren't right. You aren't wrong either. It's not about understanding the opposite perspective, but the perspective in the middle. The world is full of gray areas. So much gray, you will learn that gray is not dreary. It is a connecting point. It is an intersection. People who look for intersections tend to be happier people.

20. Just because you don't like something doesn't mean that it is bad. Like change.

21. Happiness is not something you find. You have to make it. Like oatmeal.

If you can make oatmeal, you can make happiness. If you can endure change, you can make it through college and work and life. Don't let the door hit you!

NO HUGGING ALLOWED

There are reasons I don't hug. I'm a cyborg. I like personal space. I wasn't raised with public displays of affection. There were other forms of affection in my family.

Happiness was laughter and stories at dinner time.

Protection was in the boundaries my parents set. I could play in my neighbor's yard, but no further.

Trust was in the freedom my parents gave me. I could stay out until dark; sometimes I'd only be as far away as the deck. Near or far, I could feel the love coming from my house. But we weren't a family of huggers.

With age, I've come to accept hugs and initiate hugs. I used to think it was a Southern thing, but when I got to California I met a lot of huggers out there too. One of my college roommates is from Stockton, California. She's an Olympic hugger. I can remember the first time she hugged me. It was a big embrace. Body heat and strong arms. Then right at the end, when you think the hug is done, she adds an extra squeeze that's a bit like liftoff.

It's in her blood. Her entire family gives good hugs. I know because I have hugged all of her relatives. I'm sure they wondered about my limp-fish hugs.

My friends know I'm not a hugger. I won't reject a hug, but I usually don't make the first move. There are certain times of the year where I let the hugs flow freely, but even then, the ritual of hugging is strange to me.

The deeper reason that I don't like hugging is that I'm an empath. This means I'm sensitive to other people's emotions. There was an episode of *Star Trek* (The Original Series) called "The Empath" with a lady who could take away your pain. This is great if you have a little cut on your head. But then Dr. McCoy is almost tortured to death, and the empath's healing powers save him and almost kill her.

This is sort of what I feel like when I hug people.

In addition, I have Vulcan tendencies. The mind meld is a powerful thing. Just imagine if mid hug, I reached up and put five of my fingers on your face. This would seem strange to you, but to me it's no weirder than the full body contact hug. While we are invading each other's personal space, I should at least be allowed to read your mind.

Instead of doing the limp-fish hug or the awkwardly run and hide away, I now announce with an extended hand that I'm an empath with a hint of Vulcan. People gladly shake my hand.

I give a great handshake. I have freakishly big hands. They are never sweaty or warm. They are strong hands that are cold, like a cadaver. It's like I've reached from the grave to say, "Hello. Nice to meet you."

Who wouldn't want to shake my hand?

My curse is in my children. They love to hug. All. The. Time. Extended awkward hugs. Sweaty, hot, sticky. Followed by kisses. My indifference is like a gravitational pull. Huggers sense me from a distance. They seek me out to try to ensnare me in their embrace.

To complicate matters, I love a European hug that comes with a kiss (or two or three) on the cheek. I love the hug with the kiss.

My neighbor approaches and gives me a hug, but then surprise, I get a kiss. I love this! Ooh la la.

When I was pregnant, every woman warned me about the belly touchers. I don't like hugs, why would I want people touching my basketball belly? But I loved that. If someone looked longingly at me when I was pregnant, I'd grab her hand and put in on my baby bump. It uniformly shocked everyone because of my non-hugging status, but I loved the look on someone's face when they touched my pregnant belly. They became the empaths. They took away my pain. They could feel what I feel.

A writer friend of mine died unexpectedly. She always hugged me. She didn't care if I wanted a hug or not. She gave them to me. She always had a hint of mischief in her eyes. Even though she was the same age as my mom, I always thought that we were contemporaries. Probably all the hugs.

I have lots of friends who hug me despite my hesitation. There is Pam with her red convertible. There is Tom who I see in the church parking lot. There are my little monsters.

I have lots of friends who are fine skipping the hug. There is Mamie. There is Maggie. They don't need physical proof to know that we are friends.

I needed a hug last week when my friend died. I thought that I could become a hugger, but I can't. But I'll give my hesitant hugs. I like awkward hugs. Hugs that surprise me. Kisses on the cheek. I like initiating hugs some days. I like extending a hand on other days. There are a lot of emotions radiating before and after a hug.

All of the non-huggers in the world are here to heal you. That's why you seek us out. That's why we grudgingly give you an embrace and a half-smile. We are the empaths. We are reluctant and yet grateful for your embrace.

TIME FOR MAYHEM

The entire month of May is a beatdown for parents, but I decided to take on the challenge cheerfully.

People mistakenly think I do everything. This isn't true. I only ever do the things I want to do. I hang out with my kids. I write. I go to work. This list of everything is woefully short, but I refuse to make other people feel better about their lives by listing all the things lacking in mine.

I used to think the things missing from my life included a winning lottery ticket, a maid, and 51 weeks of summer vacation. I used to think that I needed more time. "Time is the new money," they say.

Time? What the hell? If I had more time, I'd do more laundry. I don't want more time.

The month of May taught me that there is enough time. We enjoyed field day and piano recitals and graduations. If you live in the City of Decatur, your child has the opportunity to graduate from Pre-K, third grade, fifth grade, eighth grade, and 12th grade.

Do the math. I have four kids. On any given year, for the next 13 years, I will be attending two graduations. I did it cheerfully this year. I can't vouch for what I'll do in the year 2028.

The month of May taught me that there is a time for

anger. Sometimes you find out that you're a terrible parent in May. My daughter's ballet recital arrived, and I was ready. I have very few life skills, but I know how to turn 3 feet of hair into a perfect ballet bun. Hair oil, mousse, Aqua Net, 2 black hair ties, 1 hair net, 17 bobby pins.

Imagine my surprise when we get to the recital and the other four year olds are wearing tap shoes.

Who wears tap shoes to a ballet recital? In my defense, it is a dance class that occurs in the middle of the day at daycare. I never laid eyes on the teacher until the recital. In May. The month of despair.

I calmly asked the teacher, "Why are they wearing tap shoes?"

She responded in a voice like Snow White, "It's a tap and ballet class."

I've been at this daycare for 11 years. Eleven f-@%ing years. It has always been ballet. Only ballet. I take a breath. The young teacher looked like Cinderella. There were small birds flitting around her head, and two mice were peeking out of her pockets. I was about to attack her like NeNe attacked Kim on the Real Housewives of Atlanta tour bus.

But I take another breath.

"She's been in class since September. Did you ever send a note to ask for tap shoes? What has she been doing all year?"

This is 20 minutes before show time.

"She's been learning tap in her ballet shoes. I didn't send a note."

She did not send a note. I am thinking curse words in a Baptist church.

"If you had sent a note, in September, I would've sent shoes." I say this calmly. In my mind, I shout this. I hate May. I really hate May. Fortunately, the fairy princess ballet (and tap) teacher had an extra pair of shoes.

I have unfriended May.

One of the teachers at the elementary school joked that May was mayhem. I didn't laugh. Too true to be funny. May like mayday. Help me, I'm drowning. Then I remember on the other side of May is a month called June. June, like June Rose. June meaning youth. Like Juno, the protector.

I endured the third grade recorder concert. A recorder is the cross between a flute and a clarinet. It is a cheap wind instrument made by the hands of the devil and given freely to third and fourth grade children to hasten puberty.

We made a rule that playing the recorder in the car is not allowed. I try not to hate the recorder with the passion of a thousand suns. But I do. I have children who play the piano and electric guitar with amp inside my house, so I have no fear of upsetting noises. But the recorder tickles the crazy part of my brain. The recorder is May's theme song.

Here is a little known fact: Large groups of third graders playing the recorder are the reason winter is coming to Westeros. Strangely enough White Walkers can only be defeated by dragonglass, Valyrian steel, and a third grader with a recorder.

It is with some sadness that my May played out like an episode of *Game of Thrones*. I needed to wash it down with a shot of bourbon and an episode of Barney.

Remember when the worst thing in life was Barney, the creepy dinosaur? Those were the glory years.

Then I'm in June. I love June. Juno of youth. Juno, the protector. There's a girl down the street named Juno. How lucky she is that her parents didn't name her May.

I'm like Olaf the snowman. I love summer and sun and all things hot. It is May that comes in like a lamb and goes out like a lion.

May teaches you to despise the school year.

Bye, bye May.

Bye, bye recitals and class projects and graduations and school year. For seven weeks, we will miss school. On the eighth week, we will despise summer the way we now despise May. By the eighth week, we will want school back like a bad boyfriend. But for now goodbye, May. It's summer!

TOMBOY

When I was a girl, they called me a tomboy because I liked digging in the dirt. I preferred baseball caps to crinoline.

I still feel the same great affection when I see rolly pollies or fireflies. After it rains, I will stop on the sidewalk and scoot worms off the pavement and safely back into the damp earth. The rain and the dirt and insects and crawly things were my first friends.

It did not occur to me until I got older that the term "tomboy" was a kind of insult. It suggested that I was a deviant form of a girl. But I wasn't. I was 100 percent girl. I loved Barbies and romance novels and mowing the lawn and catching fireflies.

I was lucky. I never doubted who I was. I never felt pressured to conform to things I am not.

I always thought it was better to be a girl than a boy. I always thought I could be anything. Princess or gravedigger.

I never stuffed my bra or snuck behind my mother's back to wear makeup. Honestly, those things could have helped me during the awkward years. My bra stayed empty until I had babies. Then I gained breasts. No wonder men like them. They are fabulous. So soft and warm and inviting. But four breastfed babies later, my bra is as empty as it was when I was 13. I don't feel less of a woman.

I was at a meeting when someone brought up Caitlyn Jenner. I had not spared a thought on the topic since the story broke, but I instantly felt my guard go up not knowing the kind of comments my colleagues would make.

Here is the truth. I do not care.

I don't mock her. I don't disparage her. I don't overtly advocate her. Maybe I have a malaise when it comes to celebrity news. I don't care unless I think someone might say something hateful or mean. I'm not one to keep my mouth shut, so I'd rather people play nice so I can play nice.

My colleagues were appropriately positive and vague with their approval. I took a breath. I could stand down.

It made me realize that not caring might be the best thing. I do not care what kind of man or woman teaches my kids or becomes my neighbor or cooks a meal for me. I don't screen my friends to ensure their religion and politics align with mine.

Through the magic of social media I've discovered that my friends, dear close friends, are often my political and religious opposites. They remain my friends because they are kind and they work hard. They are my friends because they like to laugh and might save an earthworm every now and then.

I do not disparage the rich. I don't despise or idolize Caitlyn Jenner. I don't envy those in the spotlight. It burns.

But I do wonder what makes a woman.

By all standards only my uterus makes me one. I avoid pinchy shoes and mascara and having breasts. I don't have any interest in nail polish. Once a year I venture into Miss Nails Salon on Church Street. Tina is the owner. She has known me for 15 years. She knows I get my nails done once a year, against my will, for some fancy function.

"You going on vacation or to a wedding?" she'll ask. She knows me. "I'll do your eyebrows, too."

The year I was married, she tried to wax every bit of hair off my body.

"Like baby?" she asked.

No, not like baby. Like a woman. Leave some turf behind,

please.

I still feel fully like a woman with my crazy eyebrows and stubbly legs. I feel pretty without makeup and nail polish. There are other days when I feel pretty in a dress. There are days when I feel powerless in a world that likes to marginalize those with different skin, reproductive organs, and appearances.

I do care, and I don't care. More often than not, I don't care. This doesn't mean I won't rise to someone's defense. It doesn't mean I won't judge you for that left turn during right turn hours. It matters to me what you do with the earthworms after the rain.

That's how I know I'm a human. And a woman. And a person. Just like you.

AT THE POOL

My first memory is of drowning. I was 4 years old. We lived in Connecticut. There was a pool down the street. I remember walking right up to the glistening water. I knew it wasn't the same as solid ground, but nothing about the reflecting pool suggested danger. Or death.

I remember falling in. I don't know if I fell in accidently or if I purposely reached toward the water. I remember going under. I remember looking up.

There was light above me, and my proper life was up there.

I was sinking fast. I didn't know the concept of swimming, but I understood death. I knew I was dying and the water was going to kill me. I don't remember any emotions except the sunshine through the water.

My neighbor saved me. Her name was Mrs. Henry. I cannot remember what her face looked like or her hands. Don't remember if she had to jump into the water or if she was able to grab me near the surface. I do remember this: Being drawn to light is what almost drowned me and what certainly saved my life.

When we moved to Georgia, pools were plentiful. Our neighbors had a pool. My best friend had a pool. There was one birthday party where we had to put on as many clothes as we could and jump into the pool. I was 8 years old. We put on layers of t-shirts and sweaters and old men's suits. It seemed like a terrible idea to me, but the other kids and the parents seemed to think the game was fun.

"You can walk across the shallow end," someone said. "You don't have to swim. You'll be fine."

I believed them.

I tried to take a step through the water. But the weight of the wet clothes pulled me under. I don't remember seeing anything. I just remember feeling angry. A mom saved me because I wasn't brave enough to say no.

I was never susceptible to peer pressure after that. I never snuck out of the house. I didn't fall prey to the wiles of my boyfriend. I learned from a very young age about people. People are dangerous. The ones who let go of my hand near the water when I was 4 years old. The ones who said jump into the pool even though I wasn't a strong swimmer.

People were dangerous. Not the water. Not the pool party.

My mother has always been a practical woman. She never allowed me the chance to be afraid of water. That same year she sent me to swimming lessons at SwimAtlanta. I knew to respect the water. I knew to trust the water to lift me up. It's like a real lesson in faith and life. If you believe you can float you can. That's it. The science of your body never changes. Sinking is easy. You have to work to stay at the surface and swim.

My mom didn't learn to swim until she was in her 60s. Many summers ago, she stood next to my husband at the edge of the pool.

"I'll race you," she said to him.

My dad and I laughed when they both dove in. We've never seen a slower race.

Time moves differently when you are in the water. Time slows down, and our movements are deliberate. When we exit the water, returning to solid ground takes time. Our legs can't take the weight of gravity.

My kids aren't old enough for pool time to be fun and relaxing for me. I am sensitive to stories about tragedies at the pool. I remember being the child who wanted to touch the water. I remember being the 8 year old who couldn't swim. I remember being at the pool where others looked at me like I didn't belong.

All too often, I remember being the only black girl at the pool party. There were questions.

"Are you afraid of the water?" No. I respect it.

"Can you swim?" Yes.

"What happens to your hair?" It gets wet. Like yours. Then I wash it. Like you.

"What happens to your skin? Do you get tan?" Logically, you can't go from brown to tan. You go from brown to a darker shade of brown. Most of the time I would say, "Yes, I get tan."

No place for logical conversations in the summertime.

I spent my summers in the sun with my best friends. I applied lemon juice to my hair. I rubbed baby oil on my legs so they'd get brown faster. I knew when people were watching me like I didn't belong. I've had a lifetime of those stares. The stares started at the pool.

Almost drowning is the thing that has saved me most of my life. I can handle the stares. I can dodge the ridiculous questions. Understand the dangers of this world in the water and out.

I might have been the only black girl at the pool, but I looked down at my legs feeling proud. Like my body was the only one truly ready for summer. Like I was the only one who knew that water was a gift.

These days, I hang out in the shade. I have an umbrella. I wear a sunhat and sunglasses. I rarely go in the water. My kids wonder if I can swim. I wonder the same. I've spent a decade sitting next to the pool. A decade of babies and breastfeeding and mommy body issues. The water is a memory. I'm waiting for the right moment to dive in again.

RED FLAGS

When nine people are murdered in their place of worship, the problem isn't South Carolina. The problem isn't guns or mental health issues. The problem isn't the lack of education that first causes subtle biases and later hatred.

The problem isn't the rebel flag.

The problem is believing that racism is some distant concept that lives only in South Carolina. A lot of people unknowingly contribute to racism in America. The problem is thinking that you aren't part of the problem when you are.

When I arrived at Stanford, the first student I met asked, "What was it like growing up in Georgia? It's such a racist place."

She'd never been to Georgia. She was from Southern California. I was from Stone Mountain, Georgia the rebirth place of the Klu Klux Klan. I considered myself shy as a young adult. Shy, but not soft spoken.

"How does it feel to come from the home of the Rodney King riots?" I asked.

I did not experience overt racism growing up. Maybe I felt different. I knew when I was being watched at the pool, but no one ever called me the N-word. I've even seen a Klan march once. They held up traffic on Memorial Drive one Saturday when I was a kid. The cops on duty were both black and white. There were no spectators except those of us trying to get to Northlake Mall that afternoon.

My college roommate attended a high school with one black student. It was one of those fancy Southern California private schools that had a "The" in front of the name. Her parents were both doctors. Psychiatrists. She smoked pot. On weekends her boyfriend would drive up so they could have sex in the common room. She thought I was backwoods.

She saw no irony in the lack of diversity in her life or in her attempts to follow every spoiled-girl cliché in the book. I learned about racism from her.

I learned about racism on a business trip to Manhattan as an adult. When I entered the office of the publisher, I spoke to the receptionist while we waited for our meeting to start. I have the habit of talking to receptionists and servers at weddings and maintenance men in hotels.

"You are the first black person I've ever seen go into a meeting with Mr. Smith," she said in a whisper. "I've worked here 20 years." She smiled at me proudly. In the distance, I could see the water of the Upper Bay and the Statue of Liberty.

That night we dined in the city. Mr. Smith sat next to me. I was the only person of color, any color, in the entire restaurant. Usually there is the busboy or the lady in the coat check or someone in the kitchen who looks like me. Someone Asian or Mexican or Indian or something. There was nothing but a sea of white faces. For all of my uncomfortable moments in life, it was the first time I knew with certainty that racism was not a Southern thing.

It is easy to blame Bubbas and rednecks, but what about communities absent of diversity by exclusion? I never experienced true racism until I got to San Francisco and New York. Maybe those cities would reject the idea that they are racist, but as I've moved into adulthood I've developed a new awareness of what racism looks like.

When I moved back to Atlanta, we had a period of time when we were looking for a church to attend. We visited black churches. We visited white churches. We visited integrated churches which meant a handful of black people at a white church or a handful of white people at black church.

We visited a church in Decatur several times. Each Sunday, we filled out the visitor form and said we'd like a call or visit from the pastor. Each week, no call came. On the final Sunday we attended, an old woman in the church turned to us during the welcome portion of the service. As we shook hands she said, "You know there are a lot of other nice churches in Decatur."

I was not welcome in their house of worship. I understand. Racism is quietly everywhere. Well, get out your rebel flag. Wave it on Sundays and Saturdays and during Wednesday night Bible study.

Don't talk to me about South Carolina. Don't talk to me about guns. Or the Confederate flag. There are other ways racism is perpetuated that are more subtle and dangerous. I've seen the red flags.

I don't need everyone to love each other and hold hands and sing "Kumbaya." We don't have to all get along.

We do need to stop lying to ourselves about where racism hides and what to do when it shows its face. The face of racism is born out of a lifetime of being separate by convenience, by choice, for comfort. In New York, in L.A., in Atlanta.

I'd like you to tell me why I was the only black person at your wedding and garden party. Tell me why you don't have any Jewish friends. Tell me why you don't read books by Asian authors. Tell me why you don't like Indian food, then explain further that you've never tried it.

Don't tell me about South Carolina. Don't tell me who you voted for. Don't tell me about that red flag while ignoring the others. Tell me about your life and how we are the same and where we can find intersections. I will listen. I will believe you.

INFORMATION AND CONTACTS

Thank you for purchasing this book. We hope you enjoyed it, and if so, you might also like Nicki Salcedo's novel *All Beautiful Things*.

Locally-sourced news and current content like *Intersections* can be found on Decaturish.com every day.

We appreciate any reviews you may leave on bookseller websites. These reviews are helpful in many ways to authors seeking to make a living through writing. Again, thank you.

For more information on book releases, upcoming appearances, cat stories, time travel, and laundry battles:

Website: http://www.nickisalcedo.com/
Facebook: https://www.facebook.com/authornickisalcedo
Twitter: @NickiSalcedo
Instagram: @NickiSalcedo6

ACKNOWLEDGEMENTS

Thanks to Shane Milburn for being my genius and guide. This book would not exist without his creative and technical expertise.

Thank you to Dan Whisenhunt for trusting me with his readers and encouraging me to write the words.

Thank you to Dena Mellick for her editorial guidance, for meeting me in intersections, and for being a good neighbor.

Thanks to my mom and family and friends who have encouraged me in my non-fiction writing. Fiction is easy. Fiction is safe. The truth is difficult. My truth is not your truth. The truth changes over time.

Thanks to wonderful readers of Decaturish who encourage me to laugh and cry and question without any shame. I'm still growing. I'm still learning. I'm still listening.

ABOUT THE AUTHOR

Nicki Salcedo is an Atlanta native. She is a novelist, blogger, and a working mom. Chances are good she is the room parent for your child's class at school, and she is doing a terrible job.

She has a degree in English and Creative Writing from Stanford University. Despite her West Coast education, she considers herself Southern by sensibility, if not by birth. Southern things include talking to ghosts, saying hello to strangers, and waving to drivers with nice manners. Nicki is active in Atlanta's writing community, and her debut novel is a romantic suspense called *All Beautiful Things*.

She loves her four kids and husband, *Star Trek*, football, poetry, church, romance novels. She will never ask for your permission or forgiveness. She finds something in common with just about every person she meets. That's the untold story. That's why she writes.

ABOUT THE EDITORS

Dan Whisenhunt is an Alabama boy who moved to Atlanta. He thinks he'll stay put for awhile.

He cut his teeth as a journalist with the Anniston Star in Anniston, Alabama. He spent four wonderful years there, three as a reporter and one as an assistant editor. After that, he worked at the Times Free Press in Chattanooga, Tennessee as the county government reporter. From there, he moved to Reporter Newspapers in Sandy Springs, Georgia, where he worked as assistant editor and digital content manager.

He started Decaturish.com, locally-sourced news, as a personal project done in his spare time.

He wanted to create an environment where the contributors will not hear the word "no" when they want to try something new. He believes the news should be interesting and innovative. Decaturish.com continues to be a trusted source for information around Decatur, Atlanta, and beyond.

-

Dena Mellick is Associate Editor of Decaturish.com. Dena has worked in both local and national TV news, including Fox 5 Atlanta and CNN. She holds a Bachelor of Arts in Journalism from the University of Georgia and a Master of Theological Studies from Emory University.

She lives in Decatur, GA with her husband and two (usually misbehaving) dogs.

CPSIA information can be obtained at www.ICGtesting.com
Printed in the USA
LVOW11s1349090516

487371LV00005B/197/P